Dr. HOLT CLARKE

I DO EVER AFTER

Living Heart 2 Heart in Marriage

Cover Design by Meella

Imagination 2 Creation Publishing

Charleston, SC USA

Books by Imagination 2 Creation Publishing may be ordered through
booksellers or by contacting:

Imagination 2 Creation Publishing
www.HoltClarke.com

Because of the dynamic nature of the Internet, any web addresses or
links contained in this book may have changed since publication and
may no longer be valid. The views expressed in this work are solely
those of the author and do not necessarily reflect the views of the
publisher, and the publisher hereby disclaims any responsibility for
them.

ISBN: 978-0-9979888-5-7

To my wife Jackie.

For your steadfast love, inspiring faith, and unwavering support.

I love you!

We loved with a love that was more than love.

~ Edgar Allan Poe, *Annabel Lee*

Also Available As An Audiobook

I DO EVER AFTER

Living Heart 2 Heart in Marriage

DR. HOLT CLARKE

Wedding Minister and Marriage Coach

Introduction

Happily Ever After is not a fairy tale. It's a choice.

— Fawn Weaver, *Happy Wives Club*

Let's face it. Marriage is not for the faint of heart. And we're discovering that it's just as easy to fall out of love as it is to fall in love. The reality is that a marriage without commitment is not going to last.

An unknown source wrote, "Commitment means staying loyal to what you said you were going to do long after the mood you said it in has left."

The marriage that goes the distance is one where two people live out the promise of 'I do' through both good times and bad. They possess the grit of real love. And getting divorced is never an option.

A marriage that goes the distance is one that has at its core, a commitment and determination by two people to endure marital hardship with effective communication, collaboration, and compromise.

As a destination wedding minister in Charleston, South Carolina, I officiate lots of wedding ceremonies every year. I can't tell you how many times I see the all-too-familiar signage, 'Happily Ever After' posted in one place or another at a wedding venue. It's a nice thought, isn't it?

Many marry the love of their life and excitedly walk off together into the sunset of their happily ever after. But then something happens along the way. Setbacks, disappoints, and marital spats become all too real. The sun begins to set on their happily ever after and the darkness of divorce becomes a tempting thought. Disenchantment and disillusionment settles over the heartland and stormy eyes begin to view the wedding portrait in a different light.

Numerous things can happen to upset the integrity of a couple's happily ever after, such as: a collision of values, disagreements over finances, emotional disconnectedness, and familial wars. But what are the root causes of a marriage that goes from the fireworks and sparklers of a wedding celebration to an abysmal and often ugly cat fight of a divorce? Losing your one and only, the love of your life, and your soul mate to divorce is a bitter pill to swallow. It is the sad, common reality that happens more often than not.

Marriage is not something to dabble in. You're either all in or all out. There are too many dabblers in relationships who commit themselves whole-heartedly to the wedding planning and big day celebration but then half-heartedly commit themselves to the marriage. Values are misplaced and turned upside down. When the wedding party is over and reality sets in, far too many partners who once reveled so heartily and merrily during their wedding day, bail out of the marriage as soon as the relationship is not meeting expectations.

Losing faith in love will put you on a head trip that for some can last a lifetime. Divorce rates for second and third marriages are high. Learned behavior has a way of repeating itself. Bad habits die hard and if a couple doesn't do their due diligence by identifying triggers that lead to destructive relationship patterns, then the 'I do' of their wedding promise will quickly degenerate into 'I do NOT', culminating in divorce.

The most important investment decision you will make is choosing the partner you will spend the rest of your life with. What could be more important than choosing your partner in marriage, the one with whom you will invest your love, time, resources, career aspirations, hopes, and ultimate legacy? So getting it right in marriage is essential.

There is no perfect partner. Love is primarily a commitment of the will and secondarily a feeling of the heart. So when you ultimately choose who you will marry, do so knowing that it will involve a commitment to remain married as well.

Your marriage is what you make of it, so it's important to nurture your relationship, to bring out the best in your partner and yourself. It will take involvement and dedication, an iron will to keep saying 'I do' to your partner, and a gritty determination to fortify a love that can weather any storm life will blow your way.

I Do Ever After, is written as a hands-on premarital counseling and marriage coaching resource, providing practical insights and relational empowerment for marriage partners. It really comes down to a choice; to choose to keep saying 'I do' during marriage, especially during those times when it would be so easy to give up and walk away from your partner and marriage.

My wife Jackie and I have been happily married for many years now. Our marriage is flawed with frustrations, disagreements, and disappointments. But the one common thread that holds the tapestry of our marriage together is our commitment to love each other through thick and thin, setbacks and disappointments, trials and triumphs, happiness and sadness. We choose to say 'I do' to each other each and every day of our lives. And although there are times when we say it without the exclamation mark, we still choose to love each other, enabling our love to grow, becoming even more special with each passing day.

Living heart 2 heart in marriage is the key to a couple thriving together throughout their journey in marriage. Uniting two hearts though can be challenging, difficult, and thrilling. But it's the challenges in relational being that often prove transforming: turning differences into discovery, spats into support, and resentment into rapport.

Marriage is more than a civil or religious institution. Marriage is a relationship between two people who are committed each and every day to living into what it means to say 'I do' to each other.

Marriage is where the real stuff of love is put into action by a couple striving to embody the timeless truth from the sacred book (1 Corinthians 13:4-8, 13 NIV), "Love is patient, love is kind. It does not envy, it does not boast, it is not proud. It does not dishonor others, it is not self-seeking, it is not easily angered, it keeps no record of wrongs. Love does not delight in evil but rejoices with the truth. It always protects, always trusts, always hopes, always perseveres. Love never fails. And now these three remain: faith, hope and love. But the greatest of these is love."

When two hearts are growing as one, then even a bad day is an opportunity for a beautiful relationship to shine like a rainbow breaking forth in the midst of stormy clouds. Living heart 2 heart in marriage is what an endearing love story is made of.

Love does not have to be complicated. It really is simple but we often make it stubbornly difficult. You're happily ever after doesn't have to be elusive but an enchanting reality. True love is more than a fairy tale. It is a deep, abiding love between two people who've so grown together in marriage that they become inseparable in heart and spirit.

At the end of each chapter, there are relationship-building questions to help you examine and discuss your relationship with your significant other. The KISS (Keep It Sensible & Supportive) Exercises, consist of questions that will encourage thoughtfulness, openness, and vulnerability. Speak from the heart, but consider the power of words. When discussing matters of the heart, sensitivity and tone are very important. Be honest when sharing any concerns, hopes, and dreams you may have for your marriage.

It takes two to say 'I do' on the wedding day. And it will take two to keep a marriage growing and thriving in love throughout your journey together in life.Like Vitamin B12 to the physical body, this book is designed to serve in a similar capacity, boosting relational energy that develops an immunity against relational atrophy.

So much has been written about relationships and how to succeed in marriage. You could read volumes, I could write volumes. But when it comes down to it, growing together in marriage involves a love between two people who promise one another a lifetime of love. It is the stuff of real love, a love promised on your wedding day with two simple words, 'I do!'

Dr. Holt Clarke

Charleston, South Carolina

September 28, 2016

Chapter 1

Heart 2 Heart

The beginning of love is to let those we love be perfectly themselves, and not to twist them to fit our own image. Otherwise we love only the reflection of ourselves we find in them.

—Thomas Merton, *No Man Is An Island*

The Ohia tree in Hawai'i is one of the few plants and typically the first to grow on lava rock after new lava flows, a tough environment for anything to grow. But it's one where the Ohia tree flourishes. A beautiful flower known as the red Lehua blossom grows on its branches. The Ohia tree thrives in an environment where many other kinds of vegetation are unable.

There is a Hawaiian legend told about Ohia and Lehua who were lovers. One day the volcano goddess Pele came along and her eyes fell upon Ohia desiring him for herself. When he refused her advances, she worked her powerful magic turning him into a twisted, ugly tree. Lehua was devastated. Unable to reverse Pele's magic, the gods instead turned Lehua into a beautiful red flower and placed her on the tree so that she could always be with her beloved husband.

Legend says that when someone plucks the Lehua blossom from the tree it will rain as Lehua weeps when apart from her husband. But when a blossom is left to bloom and grow on the Ohia tree, the weather is sunny and pleasant, a sign of Ohia's and Lehua's ever blossoming and flourishing love.

Marriage is not unlike the legend of Ohia and Lehua. It really does come down to a matter of the heart. When two hearts are deeply connected, beat as one, and long to be together, a powerful bond is forged that enables and empowers love to grow in environments where many faint hearts grow weak and die.

Living heart 2 heart in marriage is made possible when two people are devoted to each other and committed to saying 'I do' to marriage long after the wedding celebration has ended. Beverley Nichols wrote, "Marriage is a book of which the first chapter is written in poetry and the remaining chapters in prose."

Making a promise to live together within an exclusive marital relationship is one of the most important decisions you will make in life. It can be a daunting choice for anyone who hasn't given thoughtful consideration to the implications. Emotions are a powerful factor in decision making. But tempering emotion with reason is what many couples fail to do before taking the marital leap. The sad reality is that often the biggest consideration a couple makes is the cost of the wedding celebration, who will pay for it, and where to go for the honeymoon. A fleeting thought at best, by far too many when planning their wedding, is given to the marriage.

The wedding industry is booming with nearly 2.5 million weddings every year in the United States, and has grown into a business empire of over $40 billion per year. And the divorce attorneys are staying just as busy.

As a destination wedding minister, I typically arrive at a gathering for a wedding in plenty of time prior to the start of the ceremony. There is ample time for me to walk around, observe, and interact with the bridal party, friends, and guests who are present for what is often a grand spectacle.

Often, I sense the excitement, the emotional charge, and the feel good spirit that is typical of a wedding celebration. Everything is carefully planned and orchestrated resulting in a grand production for a dream wedding. Friends and family are all dressed in their finest attire, the reception is exquisite and the celebration is nothing short of spectacular. All the money spent, all the time invested, and all the planning executed, comes together nicely for a charming and splendid wedding production.

With professional wedding planners in place, the bride and groom is on auto-pilot. Everything is being managed and handled for them by the professionals. The wedding preparation, planning, and execution is overseen by a professional planner who is hired to hold your hand and do your bidding every step of the way leading right up to the aisle runner. During the wedding ceremony you even have a wedding officiant prompting you with all the right answers.

What relationship wouldn't thrive in such a setting and for such a short period of time. It's easy to get along when you're both following the same script.

The wedding celebration pivots around the bride and groom saying there 'I do' during the wedding where both usually get all giddy and then later in the evening drive off together into their happily ever after. After the big kiss there is lots of applause, paparazzi, champagne, wedding cake, and your own personal DJ with the perfect mix of music to create just the right mood for the occasion.

And then a night filled with two lovers caught up in the throes of passionate love-making at a romantic honeymoon setting beneath a starry night sky. Everything for the moment seems perfect.

But then something happens along the way to happily ever after when the relational sizzle begins to fizzle. The enthusiasm and excitement of saying 'I do' begins to wane as reality sets in, life happens, and setbacks discourage star-crossed lovers. The promise of 'I do' becomes an unrealistic notion when a married couple begins to question just what they were saying 'I do' to.

How can a marriage fail after a wedding goes so well? What is the catalyst for bringing everything to a screeching halt between two people who seemed so truly, madly, and deeply in love with each other? How does a couple keep saying 'I do' to each other beyond the wedding day bliss, and avoid becoming a divorce statistic?

Although there are no magical solutions or pat answers for marital success, there are measures you can take to position your relationship with your significant other for marital health and longevity. Developing healthy relational habits is essential to maintaining a strong and vital relationship. But it takes commitment, determination, and a concerted effort by two people living heart 2 heart in marriage.

After many years of marriage, sometimes my wife and I feel as if we're pushing a barrel of concrete uphill while pushing on opposite sides of the wheel barrow. We love, laugh, and fight together. Like Noah and Allie in the movie, *The Notebook*, it's what we do at times. It's what healthy relationships do. But the key – is that we are together, not apart, and that's how we make our marriage thrive. We do it together.

So how do you move together, heart 2 heart, in the same direction with your partner, when you both bring to the table different ideas, desires, experiences, and dreams? How do you create and sustain a synergy that is cohesive and empowering for your marriage?

The first step on the journey toward relational harmony is learning to get back to the basics of love. What does it mean to truly love another more than you love yourself? What does that kind of self-giving love look like, how is it expressed, and how does it flourish in marriage?

Love means different things to different people. Learning to talk to your partner about what he/she thinks love is, begins a very interesting conversation regarding matters of the heart. Defining love and picturing what it looks like is a great relational exercise to undertake together. You'll be amazed at what you will learn and uncover about each other in the process.

Some people tend to define love using concrete language that is sensory related and has to do with emotions and romance. Others define love using abstract language that is non-sensory and rational. Love encompasses both emotion and reason. Sort of like how I describe the difference in the appeal of religion and spirituality. Religion tends to appeal to those desiring an experience of the mind. Whereas spirituality tends to appeal to those desiring an experience of the heart. One is not necessarily better than the other, but when you join the two it can be a powerfully winning combination.

Striving to be harmonious in heart and mind is no easy undertaking. It is a journey toward marital fitness that every couple must seriously take together to experience satisfying love and marital longevity. Relational harmony is achieved when a couple is able to embody love that engages both the heart and mind in the formation of a rock solid marriage, where a couple can blossom and flourish long after the hot lava flow of an argument has cooled.

Nicholas Sparks wrote, "Every couple needs to argue now and then. Just to prove that the relationship is strong enough to survive. Long-term relationships, the ones that matter, are all about weathering the peaks and the valleys."

Let's look at some practical ways a marriage between two people can weather the storms of life.

From Independence to Interdependence

We are each other's harvest; we are each other's business; we are each other's magnitude and bond.

—Gwendolyn Brooks

Growing in love as a couple involves the intentional effort of learning to think and act as one. Two are better than one if two can act as one. This doesn't mean trying to change your partner into a more fitting reflection of yourself. A relationship that is primarily defined by one partner needs to be recalibrated. A marriage involves two people and both should be working in concert to grow as one in love.

Now of course, when two people are involved there will be differences of opinion and disagreements where you will simply need to agree to disagree. But that doesn't provide a convenient excuse to jettison the ideas and input of your significant other when important decisions are to be made that will impact the marriage. To do so is to simply digress into a relationship that is akin to two monkeys throwing bananas at each other from different trees. Disagreements often require compromise for the sake of the relationship so you don't resort to throwing bananas at each other.

The breakdown in many marriages usually happens when two people stop living and loving as a couple, and revert to living and tolerating each other as roommates. We live in a time when individualism, self-reliance, and self-empowerment are pop curlture values readily embraced. And although it's psychologically healthy to bloom in one's independence outside of marriage, it can become unhealthy for two people in marriage. An independent personality that recklessly seeks to dominate a marital relationship can prove to be unhealthy, serving as an iceberg that will sink a marriage.

Cultivating a marriage where two individuals regularly assess and recalibrate so as to become less independent and more interdependent, is vital to marital sustainability. It's important to realize that a relationship characterized by interdependence takes time to cultivate and doesn't happen overnight.

Peter De Vries wrote, "The bonds of matrimony are like any other bonds — they mature slowly." It takes two people striving on a daily basis to create such synergy, that in time they find themselves almost effortlessly facing together the many frustrations, difficulties, challenges, opportunities, and celebrations that marriage will present.

Marriage is a relational journey in which two people are heading in the same direction. It's a shared journey where two people are stepping out together and finding their common stride, not as two individuals but as one couple. Learning to live, love, and laugh as one, is essential to cultivating a relationship that evolves into a marriage characterized by two hearts beating as one.

If you remain fixed in an independent mind set early on in a marriage, the chances of growing in love as a healthy couple will be minimal. Rather than co-existing as two independent people living under one roof, marriage necessitates that two people pool together their intellectual, spiritual, emotional, and material resources. If you stubbornly cling to your independence during a marriage you'll soon discover yourself living alone.

Harmonizing in Marriage

When we feel, a kind of lyric is sung in our heart. When we think, a kind of music is played in our mind. In harmony, both create a beautiful symphony of life.

— Toba Beta

Just as a body needs the the heart and brain to thrive in health, so two people need each other to thrive in marriage. A happy, healthy marriage requires harmony of heart and mind. A meaningful and fulfilling marriage consists of two people who are serious about making their relationship work. Their marriage is a priority and doesn't play second fiddle to anything else.

I'm an eclectic music lover and as such I appreciate music that creatively blends melodious sounds, harmonizing vocals, and meaningful lyrics. The creation of blended music is the result of an inspired process that began with imaginative thought, collaborative effort, and musical instruments. Just picking up a violin and thrumming the strings without understanding how to play the instrument is not going to produce inspiring music; but rather earsplitting noise. You must first understand how to hold the instrument, how to touch the instrument, how to tune the instrument, and how to harmonize an instrument, before creating a sound pleasing to the ear.

Much in the same way, a couple begins making music together

when they master the process of thinking, collaborating, and harmonizing together. Two people are like instruments and when harmonized, create an ear-pleasing melody. Learning to harmonize as a couple is key to making soulful music together. But before you can start harmonizing together you've got to learn how to make music that is inspiring and edifying to your marriage.

Like musical instruments, you and your partner must invest the necessary time to learn everything there is to know about the other. Don't assume that the courtship has garnered you sufficient information about your partner. Admiring the beauty of an instrument and producing melodious sounds from an instrument, are two different animals entirely.

Taking your partner for granted by making false assumptions as a result of not getting to know your partner will result in some less than delightful sounds. The noise created will cause you both to invest in earplugs so as to shut each other out. Unhappy instruments make unhappy sounds.

Take the time to get to know your partner. This will require an investment of your mind and heart to: listen, learn, share, observe, and love. Master musicians are not created overnight. And neither are marriages that last.

The sad reality is that many recklessly make the marital leap due to infatuation, insecurity, or financial security. Love often has little if anything to do with it. Many couples spend very little time discussing what love truly is, how it flourishes, and where they hope it will take them in marriage. And when things start to go south usually one or both individuals in the relationship are ready to jettison the marriage out of frustration, discontent, or insecurity. Thus the reason why second marriages have a higher rate of divorce than first marriages and third marriages have a higher rate of divorce than second marriages. The vicious cycle keeps repeating and recreating itself.

It's so important to get it right the first time around by spending time learning how to make music together. And like any instrument, realized that your marriage will need to be tuned periodically for the best quality sound and listening enjoyment. Learning practical ways to fine tune your marriage is key to making love blossom and flourish in marriage.

Learn to Garden

People are like dirt. They can either nourish you and help you grow as a person or they can stunt your growth and make you wilt and die.

—Plato

I still believe in chivalry, when people chose to do the right things, for the right reasons, at the right times. On one occasion prior to the start of a wedding I was to officiate, I overhead a groomsman offer the groom some advice. He simply said, "Happy wife! Happy life!" Although a bit of a cliché there is some truth to those words.

My wife loves to garden and because of such, I've grown to develop an appreciation for gardening. Before we met, I had zero interest in gardening. It's the last thing I would've ever considered taking up as a hobby. But our marriage gave me a newfound appreciation for gardening.

Over the years, I've grown to appreciate and enjoy those moments working alongside my wife as we tend our garden together. In the beginning, I was less than thrilled to get my hands dirty doing something when I felt there were more important things I could be doing with my time. But when I stopped thinking about my time and began considering my wife's time and how she enjoyed spending it, I began to see gardening in a new light.

Gardening is an activity that brings peace, relaxation, and pleasure to my wife. Her senses are exhilarated by the process of tilling the soil, planting seeds, watering, and weeding the garden. And when the vegetables and herbs begin to sprout and grow she gets even more thrilled and engaged in the gardening experience.

Initially I was like, "Wouldn't it be so much simpler to just go buy these veggies and herbs at a store?" My thinking was limited to expedience rather than a shared experience. I soon discovered that the experience of gardening together was a boon to our marriage. The more I participated in the gardening experience with her the more she enjoyed casting a fishing line in the ocean with me.

My wife and I now share a love for gardening together because I took the time to discover and participate in an activity that my wife enjoys. Discovering and sharing in your partner's interests will broaden your own and help to take your marriage from good to great! The result of shared experiences is an enrichment of your marriage.

Ann Landers wrote, "Love is friendship that has caught fire. It is quiet understanding, mutual confidence, sharing and forgiving. It is loyalty through good and bad times. It settles for less than perfection and makes allowances for human weaknesses."

Fundamental to Gardening 101, is the fact that seeds can remain dormant if environmental conditions are not conducive to growth. In a similar way, some marriages are like dormant seeds that fail to germinate because psychological, relational, and environmental conditions are simply not suitable for germination. The best way to cultivate healthy marital soil is by getting to know your partner and not assume anything.

Cultivating a healthy marriage is not much different than cultivating a healthy garden. Every marital relationship has within it the seeds of a potentially great marriage that can grow and flourish in love. The challenge is to discover what kinds of relational conditions are helpful rather than harmful to two people sowing seeds within the soil of their marriage.

A supportive partner is like nutrient-rich soil. When a partner feels understood, valued, and respected, there is not much he/she will not do to reciprocate in kind. Becoming other-centered in a relationship is the way you till the soil of a marriage. And make no mistake about it, the soil of marriage must be tilled.

The first few years of a marriage can be very challenging. When couples try to ride the coattails of the courtship, wedding, and honeymoon, they quickly discover that emotional highs last but a season and will not carry a relationship but for so long. Tilling the soil of marriage will create optimal conditions for nurturing and growing a relationship that is healthy, purposeful, and fulfilling.

Taking time to water the soil of your relationship garden is crucial to developing and sustaining a healthy marriage. This can happen when you roll over in the bed and the first thing you say to your partner in the morning is, "I love you!" It may be a much appreciated gesture of opening the car door for your partner as a display of respect and value. Or it could be a token gift that expresses your love.

In the movie, *Finding Forrester*, the character William Forrester portrayed by Sean Connery, offers the following relational advice to a young teenage prodigy. "The key to a woman's heart is an unexpected gift at an unexpected time."

The marital garden must be tended daily for love to be nurtured and given the best possible chance to grow. Otherwise the weeds will soon overtake the garden, deprive the soil of vital nutrients, and leave only poor conditions for the seeds of a marriage to sprout.

Never take your partner for granted. Be supportive and grow with your partner in love. Do this and your marriage will become like an Oak tree with deep roots, an expansive trunk, and sprawling branches.

Don't Forget to Breathe

What oxygen is to the lungs, such is hope to the meaning of life.

—Emil Brunner

One of my favorite movies is the 80's version of *The Karate Kid*. Int the movie, Miyagi, a handyman and martial arts master, befriends a young bullied teen named Daniel Laruso and teaches him karate. During the training, he often admonishes Daniel about the importance of breathing. "Don't forget to breathe. Very important." A simple and fairly basic notion, and yet so very important to one's core mental and physical strength.

Breathing is also essential to a healthy marriage, creating safe space for centering and calming the mind.

At times, breathing is hampered when a marriage catches cold and the relationship plateaus and is drained of its vitality. Pull out of these cold spells by clearing your relational air passage ways. Find what it is that excites and ignites a fire in you as a couple. Discover and experience activities that create lasting memories. Some of course, will be more memorable than others.

Jackie, my wife, had a great idea one day. She decided we were going to take up roller blading. I was like, "you've got to be kidding! I haven't put skates on since I was a kid. I really don't think this a good idea." But no siree! She was bound and determined for us to roller blade and besides, she had done this in college. I sheepishly put my skates on and immediately felt unhinged from any since of balance. I was a weeble wobble on wheels. It was a matter of moments before I went down on my knees and tumbled over. "Ok, I'm not so sure this is the best activity for us to take up," I remember saying. And then I heard groaning on the ground behind me.

While I was unstrapping my roller blades, Jackie had fallen over backwards and her arm was broken in two places along her right forearm. It was a palpable moment to say the least. Our four year old son, Luke and I, rushed mom to the hospital where she was prepped for surgery. Several hours later she came out of OR with titanium plates in her arm, stronger than before.

I'm now married to a bionic woman. And all because of her daring fervor to try something new that we had never done before as a couple. And probably never will again :-) And that's ok, because we both treasure every experience and memory we create together.

Keeping your relationship calibrated and functioning at an optimal level will require work and imagination. This is where the fun comes into play. Think about what your marriage needs to breathe freely and soundly. It may be an activity that allows you the freedom to exercise your imagination and channel your creativity. It may be require a recreational activity.

For some, breathing will require alone time that cultivates a new perspective and attitude, so that behaviors can become more conducive to a healthy, mutually reciprocal relationship. Regardless of what the activity may entail, learning to breathe in marriage is essential and conducive to flourishing in love.

KISS Exercises

(Keep It Sensible & Supportive)

Rules for Sharing:

Be Open and Honest

Do Not Judge

Respect Your Partner's Thoughts and Feelings

Love Always

1.   Share with your partner five reasons why you love him/her?

2.   What do you see as your relational strengths? Weaknesses?

3.   Share a negative experience you had in a relationship with another partner, parent, or friend? Share two words that describe your emotional response to the situation. Why did it upset you?

4.   What do you enjoy most about your relationship with your partner?

5.   Why do you desire to spend the rest of your life with your partner?

6.   Discuss with each other the promise you made to be married for the rest of your lives together.

7.   Discuss how you both will keep your marriage calibrated and functioning at an optimal level, so that your love can grow and flourish.

Chapter 2

Risking Vulnerability

If we're wrapping ourselves up to conceal any vulnerability, whatever happens to us has to go through all those extra layers. Sometimes love doesn't even reach where we truly live.

— Alexandra Katehakis, *Mirror of Intimacy*

In James Cameron's movie *Avatar*, one of the memorable lines in the movie is the greeting used by the Na'vi tribe members "I See You." The greeting did not originate with the movie but is actually the traditional greeting used by members of the Northern Natal tribes of South Africa. Their daily greeting to each other begins with "Sawa bona", which literally means, "I see you." The response is "Sikhona", which means, "I am here".

Beyond a mere "Hello", the daily greeting which states, "I See You", is more than acknowledgement of another but rather, "I understand you", "I get you", "I'm tracking with you". And to respond, "I am here" is more than a statement of existence but rather, "I am with you." "We are together on this journey." "We are in OUR zone."

Being vulnerable in an authentic relationship involves a togetherness that is secure enough to move beyond the shallow stuff, in order to get to know and understand another. There is an "I see you" component to the relationship. And when someone knows the depths of you and loves you despite the flaws, then vulnerability becomes a ray of sunshine, causing a marriage to bloom and grow.

Adopting a "we" mentality involves a healthy dose of self-denial. Not in the sense that you lose your individuality and self-identity, but rather in becoming intentional about being a couple in marriage by moving in the same direction, sharing experiences, and contributing to mutual goals. Attitudes you currently have may require: recalibration, habits to be adapted, and a new way of being to be developed. In marriage self-improvement is a segue to relationship improvement.

Modifying attitudes and behaviors is a process that involves intentional self-growth as well as relational growth. It's a paradox of sorts that begins with the person in the mirror.

Living in sync with your significant other is the result of growing in your togetherness. When you are in tune with each other, married life becomes relationally harmonious and healthy. Having less of "me" and more of "we" will make your marriage more fulfilling and sustainable. But moving beyond "me" to "we" begins with being vulnerable in marriage.

Risking vulnerability in marriage is intimidating. Fear of being judged, rejected, or even abandoned, can be frightening, especially if you've been burned in the past by disclosing something about yourself that was used against you in a hurtful manner. But learning to trust your partner is essential to growing in love.

Vulnerability leads to intimacy. Being intimate in marriage is more than having sex, it's being together and sharing experiences. It's the intimate interactions outside the bedroom that make love-making in the bedroom more special and meaningful. Intimacy presents opportunities for strengthening your relationship through shared experiences. Authentic intimacy fosters a stronger sense of self, a stronger relationship, and a stronger marriage.

Vulnerability and intimacy empowers you as a couple. Yes, intimacy can be frightening but learning to share and trust in each other is what makes a marriage last. It will challenge you to get out of your comfort zone and learn to experience your relationship in an up close and personal way. It will put the titanium in your relationship, bonding you together with a confidence from knowing that your partner sees you and loves you just as you are.

Cultivating intimacy in marriage involves the willingness of both partners to tear down the walls of self-preservation and guardedness. Fear is a dark energy that will zap you and your marriage of vitality. Most of us have been burned a time or two in life. And nothing can be more painful than being deeply hurt by a significant other. But that isn't a reason to stop trusting or believing in the power of love to make a new beginning.

A sense of connection is what binds two people together. But when you feel disconnected in marriage it's usually a result of guarding secrets. And protecting one's secrets is often driven by a fear of letting the cat out of the bag.

Jack Canfield wrote, "Everything you want is on the other side of fear." Vulnerability leads to authentic intimacy when you're willing to risk being hurt, rejected, or abandoned. Nothing is more frightening that the fear of losing someone's love. But as you become secure in your relationship you will find yourself wondering why you were afraid to risk vulnerability in the first place.

Tracie Bennett wrote, "I am so scared of the sea, so what did I do? Learned to scuba in the Great Barrier Reef." Fear is often the barrier to realizing true intimacy. But when you confront head on your dark places, you will find yourself escaping the maze of melancholy and experiencing the thrill and wonder of married life.

It's been said, "Intimacy is the act of connecting with someone so deeply, you feel like you can see into their soul." That can be a scary thought for some. But when two people have learned to trust and confide in each other, they experience a liberation that enables the marriage to flourish. There is no longer a need to wear masks. The marriage becomes liberating.

When you are fully known and fully loved by your partner and vice versa, it is freeing and empowering for you both. And when relational walls are torn down, then you both are enabled to love with confidence, knowing you're truly together on this journey called life.

I like to think of the wedding as the cocoon process of a loving relationship, and the marriage is the butterfly effect where two people emerge as one and learn to fly together. Rather than feeling frightened, caged, and under a cloud of doubt, marriage should inspire a couple to soar.

Rethinking Vulnerability

I understand now that the vulnerability I've always felt is the greatest strength a person can have. You can't experience life without feeling life. What I've learned is that being vulnerable to somebody you love is not a weakness, it's a strength.

—Elizabeth Shue

The definition of vulnerability is "to be capable of or susceptible to being wounded or hurt." Who wants to do that? Risking vulnerability goes against our very nature, the struggle for self-preservation is a powerful primal instinct. In the context of marriage, vulnerability is that leap of faith required to realize your happily ever after.

Identifying and ceasing behavioral patterns that create relational disconnectedness is essential. Often attitudes and behaviors are employed to protect from pain, but have the negative effect of obstructing healthy intimacy and sabotaging a marriage. Identifying and disarming these attitudes and behaviors requires vulnerability.

When one has experienced psychological or physical abuse by a parental figure or a significant other, defense mechanisms are employed to cope and to prevent future occurrences. But to grow in a loving marital relationship, a dismantling of emotional barriers is required. To form a real connection, experience a real friendship, and enjoy a flourishing marriage, a rethinking of vulnerability begins the process of disarming our defenses.

It's a conundrum for many. Do you risk disclosing a part of your life that your partner may dislike, and thus run the risk of abandonment? Give yourself enough time and you can find an endless number of reasons to avoid risking vulnerability with your partner. But fear is not an emotion that should be allowed to rule your life or your marriage. So cut it off at the source early in your relationship by purging fear from your life. If your partner's love is real, then his/her love is strong enough to handle it.

Vulnerability is essential to cultivating an authentic marriage. It requires that two people learn to trust each other with those sensitive and delicate matters of the heart so that healing can take place. There are no guarantees in life, but love more than any other emotion has the power to make one whole again and to empower a marriage.

Rethinking vulnerability involves opening the gates and letting another in. Two become one when both grow in their love, trust, and belief in each other. To keep thinking and behaving in guarded ways as you once did in your single life, expecting the same protective results in your marriage, is to invite relational disaster.

Vulnerability invites your partner into your safe space by opening your heart so that he or she may understand and be present. To do so when everything in you screams 'YOUR CRAZY', is the stuff that real love is made of, and the anvil upon which which real marriages are forged. The gain to be realized from such a risk is self-validation, self-liberation, psychological healing, spiritual freedom, and a greater capacity to love openly and authentically.

To be vulnerable is to know true relational strength. Vulnerability jettisons superficiality in relationships. My advice to couples that are struggling with superficiality, is to be real with one another. If you don't feel safe revealing who you truly are to your partner then you're in for an emotionally taxing and debilitating relationship.

People develop cynical attitudes and become critical when they've been burned in the past. And often this negativity is carried over into a subsequent relationship. We all have scars, wounds, failures, and disappointments that we bring to a relationship. Often referred to as 'baggage', I choose to call it diamonds in the rough. When you love your partner despite the veneer of coal, then you inspire the diamond inside to shine forth with beauty and brilliance.

Letting down your defenses in marriage is essential to feeling at peace with life. If there is no peace inside then everything tends to be filtered by your unease, uncertainty, and unbelief. Realizing your core inner strength begins with: accepting who you are, believing in who you are, and loving who you are. Only then will you enjoy the fruit of vulnerability.

It's been said that "faith pitches her tent in the valley of travail," and it's true. Marriage involves hardships. Many marriages fall apart when setbacks happen. Frustrations often mount when a sense of losing control over a situation becomes real. This is why a real sense of connectedness is so important to a healthy marital relationship. During trying times when many couples pull apart in marriage, a couple that has cultivated a strong relational core through vulnerability, will pull together.

There is nothing that you can't weather together as long as you have faith in each other. Every relationship has its moment of truth, and marriage is often when that moment of truth takes place.

Standing together, heart 2 heart, is how a couple can strengthen their relational bond through vulnerability. No walls, no pretense, no cover ups. Just good ole let your hair down, no makeup, kind of real togetherness. Au naturel vulnerability is the stuff of strong marriages where relational health, harmony, and longevity is experienced.

Mark Twain wrote, "Love seems the swiftest but it is the slowest of all growths. No man or woman really knows what perfect love is until they have been married a quarter of a century."

Vulnerability is what enables a marriage to go the distance when two people have mastered what it is to be vulnerable in love, enjoying the fruit of their love.

Rethinking vulnerability also involves courage. Carlo Alcos of the Matador Network, tells of Dr. Brené Brown, a leading researcher on vulnerability who did a study of people over a six year period. She found that most fall into two groups: those with a strong sense of love and belonging, and those who struggle with it. Those with a strong sense of love and belonging also shared something in common, courage.

Alcos wrote in his article, *The Art of Practicing Vulnerability,*

"Courage comes from the latin 'cor', meaning heart. The original definition of courage was 'to tell the story of who you are with your whole heart.'"

Relational strength stems from courage. By being courageous in love you make it possible to cultivate an honest, open, and fulfilling marriage with your partner. Courage strengthens your relationship so you both are free to be yourselves without fear of being judged or rejected.

Experiencing and enjoying emotional security in your relationship happens when you risk vulnerability and accepting the uncertainty that comes with it. Don't make assumptions. Communicate with your partner and stay connected heart 2 heart.

Saying 'I do' in marriage involves a commitment to being vulnerable to your partner in ways that may be uncomfortable and alarming. The fear of being vulnerable is palpable and is overcome by an unreserved trust and faith in a love that is real.

KISS Exercises

(Keep It Sensible & Supportive)

Rules for Sharing:

Be Open and Honest

Do Not Judge

Respect Your Partner's Thoughts and Feelings

Love Always

1.   Are there experiences in your personal life you are afraid to discuss with your partner? Professional life? If so, why?

2.   Discuss together areas of your life that make you feel vulnerable to being judged or even rejected. Unpack the reasons why?

3.   In what areas do you believe your relationship is most vulnerable?

4.   Reflect on disagreements you've had with one another since being together. Were concessions or compromises made to reach an agreement?

5.   Discuss openly and honestly your sense of "me" versus "we" in your relationship. What percentage would represent "me" and what percentage would represent "we"?

6.   What kinds of adjectives would you use to describe your relationship?

7.   Discuss what it means to trust and have faith in each other.

Chapter 3

Managing Change

God grant me the serenity to accept the things I cannot change, the courage to change the things I can, and the wisdom to know the difference.

— Reinhold Niebuhr, *The Serenity Prayer*

In some ways, preparing for marriage is similar to planning an outdoor destination wedding. You can have the best laid plans for the perfect wedding. And then come wedding day, Mother Nature decides to show up with thunder, lightning, and torrential rain in tow.

I've seen the desperation and disappointment on the faces of brides when the weather didn't cooperate on their big day. The dark clouds outside quickly drifted inside. The mood of a wedding celebration can quickly go south with the first rumble of thunder and clap of lightning.

Although it can be a bride's nightmare, inclement weather can also be a wake up call for the couple who think married life is all about sunshine and rainbows. A marriage entails the good, the bad, and the ugly, so ready or not, you better be prepared for days fraught with inclement weather.

The wedding day can be a good precursor of what to expect during a marriage. Anything from a vendor being a no show, the delivery of the wrong shade of flowers by the florist, an officiant using the wrong vows, or a family member experiencing a stroke prior to the processional. I've just about seen, experienced, and heard it all, when it comes to wedding day surprises and nightmare scenarios.

The unforeseen and unpredictable circumstances of life have a way of spoiling the best laid plans; throwing everything into a tail spin when life seems to spiral out of control. It's when life arouses a sense of powerlessness and lack of control that many seek to swim against the rip tide of change and end up relationally drowning.

Rather than pulling together, many couples pull apart when their own notions of an ideal marriage never quite materializes. During such times of frustration the temptation is to make a knee jerk reaction. Marital bliss succumbs to unmet and unrealistic expectations leading to disillusionment and disenchantment.

The Proposal

I ask you pass through life at my side—to be my second self, and best earthly companion.

—Charlotte Brontë, *Jane Eyre*

A marriage proposal is an invitation to change. Change is both exciting and frightening when two people are about to make a decision that will forever alter their lives. To say 'yes' is to say "yes" to change. And when you promise 'I do' to your partner during the wedding ceremony, you are also saying 'I do' to a lifetime of change. It would be naïve to think otherwise.

Accepting another's proposal to enter into a marital relationship is your acceptance to enter into a state of change. And when the two of you make the promise of 'I do' before friends, family, and God at your wedding, you're making a declaration that invites change into your life for better or for worse. The kind of change that is unpredictable.

Marriage is a vast ocean of unknown awaiting exploration and discovery. The thought can be intimidating as you ponder the implications of such a venture of faith. Think about it. Two people coming from different backgrounds, experiences, and family traditions. Values may be different, tastes may vary, career tracks heading in opposite directions, goals and ambitions at a crossroads, and the potential for a clash of ideas ramp up when going from single to married.

Love has a way of bringing a couple face to face with the stark reality of pledging to a lifetime of negotiating and managing change. Some do so with little thought of the implications. Others do so with great trepidation. In the end, it really comes down to a matter of choice. Choosing to step out in faith by believing in each other, believing in your love, and believing in your hopes and dreams as a couple.

During a pre-marriage coaching session I had with a couple, the groom was emphatic about his desire of not wanting anything to change between he and his fiancé when they got married. Their relationship was perfect according to him. He didn't expect his fiancé to make any changes because that was why their relationship was so ideal. The young man's naïve thinking became readily apparent although his intentions were sincere.

As I listened to the groom share I couldn't help but think to myself, 'Bless his heart. He is in for a rude awakening.'

What came to light during the course of the conversation, was the groom's fear of having to make some changes based on concerns that were deeply troubling his fiancé. By being so emphatic about not expecting his fiancé to change, he was sending the unspoken message, 'Don't expect me to change either.'

Our marriage coaching sessions provided a safe space for them to air their concerns and hear each other out. In bringing her concerns to light, she found him to be very receptive. Learning to open up and share from the heart without becoming defensive is essential to nurturing a healthy marriage.

Dealing effectively with change is essential to navigating the destructive and shallow shoals of self-centeredness. Although you will not be able to fully control change when it happens in your life, what you can control is your response to it. Sometimes a walk in the pouring rain makes you more appreciative of those sunny days. Learning to weather a stormy marriage by waiting for the weather to break, is an opportunity to share a good laugh and a cup of tea. At times, we just need to get over ourselves and laugh it off.

Exploring the effects of change can help you recognize and respond appropriately when the symptoms begin to manifest in your relationship.

Dealing with Disruption

If you don't like something, change it. If you can't change it, change your attitude.

—Maya Angelou

Change is disruptive. And some people do not deal with disruption very well. On one occasion while waiting to officiate a wedding at one of Charleston, South Carolina's beautiful plantations, I heard a scream. At first, I thought it was a tourist having a really bad day and being quite dramatic about it. It turned out to be the sister of the groom.

The event coordinator came running over and asked if I would go speak to the family and try to mitigate the situation. After about a thirty minute delay to the start of the wedding ceremony, I was able to work with the family in getting the sister to calm down enough so that the wedding could proceed.

The sister of the groom felt threatened by her future sister-in-law and resented her budding relationship with her mother and brother. The wedding hit on some emotional triggers that proved extremely upsetting and difficult for her to accept. The wedding signified to her, the end of a significant family relationship. She viewed her future sister-in-law as a relational threat. She refused to be consoled and did not relent in her objection of the wedding. She remained adamant about not attending the wedding and so reluctantly the groom made the difficult decision of proceeding without his sister in attendance.

What may seem like an extreme response, is nonetheless, a very real emotional reaction to change and the disruption it often creates in a person's life. Sometimes you may wish to escape and be secluded on a desert island to escape change.

Change happens. The only thing you can control is your attitude and response to it. Will it be a response involving kicking and screaming or one that is conducive to constructive growth? How you learn to cope with change will determine to a large extent how effectively you and your partner grow together in love. Which leads us to another difficult challenge for couples, and that is how to effectively manage conflict that often arises because of change.

Managing Conflict

The most important thing in communication is hearing what isn't being said. The art of reading between the lines is a life-long quest of the wise.

—Shannon L. Alder

Change will inevitably lead to conflict in your marriage. Count on it and be prepared to effectively deal with it. When discord erupts it has a way of causing a couple to lose a sense of relational stability. Effectively working through conflict and the tension that it often elicits in a marriage, takes emotional restraint, patience, and a willingness to listen to your partner's perspective without shutting him/her down. This can be extremely difficult to do when you're emotionally charged.

Early on in our marriage, everything about our relationship was like a cocktail with an umbrella in it. Life was was absolutely hunky dory, at least until I discovered my wife is a pack rat. I like things neat and tidy and well organized. It wasn't long into our marriage, that my OCD world came crashing down around me.

It began with the garage clutter. And then like a *Goosebumps* book, things got even scarier. Attic clutter, and the closet clutter, the cyber clutter, living space clutter, screen porch clutter, back yard clutter, front yard clutter, beneath the beds clutter, refrigerator clutter, and cupboards clutter. Yikes!

Now, in fairness to my wife, what constitutes clutter is relative. What I viewed as clutter, was sentimental and meaningful to her. I had to change my perspective to understand her sentimentality when it came to what I viewed as clutter.

I'd like to say I was initially the better man and simply adapted without grumbling and complaining, but that would be far from the truth. I put up an embattled resistance and challenged the right for order and chaos to coexist. She raised her rebel flag and flew it proudly, while I pointed to the stars and stripes and fiercely advocated for the abolition of all chaos. Although neither threatened to secede from the marital union, we learned to compromise and and make concessions. Our marriage was able to evolve encompassing both chaos and order exist under the same roof.

My wife and I find ourselves laughing together about issues that used to create major consternation. By avoiding the tendency to rush to judgment, we learned to listen to each other, hear each other out, and respect each other's values. And as a result, we've been successful in keeping our marriage skipping along our happily ever after road.

Finding common ground in the midst of discord is essential to relational harmony. Conflict can be constructive if it results in marital harmony.

Toba Beta wrote in his book, *Master of Stupidity*, "If your heart tends to force friends to do as you say, seed of discord is being planted in your relationship."

I learned an important lesson in my marriage. Trying to dictate the terms of a relationship is not how to sustain a meaningful and enduring marriage. Marriage is a relationship-intensive undertaking. And it requires give and take on both sides.

In time, I came to see my wife's clutter as an important part of her orderly world. When I stopped making false assumptions about her clutter, our marriage became less bumpy and more smooth. Marriage works best when both partners love graciously, listen generously, and laugh considerably.

Discerning Depression

When you don't understand what happens when you're depressed and you listen to everything your depressed mind says, you can cause havoc in your relationship.

—Lisa Esile

Change is often a precursor to marital depression. We often think of depression in terms of the individual but couples also can suffer from relationship depression. And recognizing when you or your partner may be suffering from depression as a result of change, is critical to effectively coping with a spectrum of possible emotional responses.

There are two primary causes of depression. One trigger of depression is what's called endogenous due to a chemical imbalance. The other trigger for depression is reactive caused by changes in your environment. Environmental factors such as a new job, death of a loved one, move to a new community etc., can often serve as a trigger for sending a marital relationship into an emotional spiral.

And marital depression often opens the door to a number of potential relationship-ending actions. Not taking the time to recalibrate during emotionally stressful times due to environmental changes will deplete vital energy from a marital relationship, and if left uncheck can prove detrimental to the marriage.

Vulnerability to extra-marital affairs is strongest when a couple feels estranged and disconnected from each other. My advice is not to neglect what you can protect. More than a cliché, it's a simple truth that will keep your marriage thriving in relational health. If you truly care about your partner and the love you both share, you will find the time to exercise preventive and restorative care.

Marriage coaching and solid relationship resources such as relational growth books and couple's retreats are means of preventive care. You should invest time and resources into protecthing and enhancing your relationship. It's a love that deserves your undivided attention. The security and stability of your family, especially if children are involved, is dependent upon your intentional efforts to do so.

Restorative care can be realized in a number of ways including professional intervention from a marriage and family therapist who is trained to assist in mending areas of your relationship that require therapeutic care. Outside professional assistance who is an objective ear and voice, can help frame relationship issues in a constructive manner.

Another important activity to help with restorative care is to have a no-technology date night. Being together without the intrusion and distration of a smart phone or social media, is vital to protecting your alone time together. You'll be amazed at just how palliative it is to create private space as a couple, when you revisit and rediscover the reasons why you first fell in love with each other.

Relationship depression can be daunting for a couple to experience. But rather than serving as a catalyst for divorce, it can be a mean of strengthening your relationship. All couples deal with bouts of depression during their marriage. Greet it as an opportunity to draw closer to your partner, and a means of bringing out the very best in each other.

When Opportunity Knocks

Trials, temptations, disappointments -- all these are helps instead of hindrances, if one uses them rightly. They not only test the fiber of character but strengthen it...Every trial endured and weathered in the right spirit makes a soul nobler and stronger than it was before.

—James Buckham

Change can create opportunity in your marriage. Change doesn't have to be the pink elephant in the room. It can be the impetus for creating positive energy and momentum in your relationship. And it can serve as the catalyst for injecting passion into your relationship; the kind that draws you closer together as a couple.

When the unforeseen happens in your life, and it will, view it as a stepping stone rather than a setback. Before allowing yourself to get hot and bothered by unsettling change, embrace it as an opportunity to experience a more fulfilling relationship as a couple.

After serving as a pastor in the United Methodist Church for fifteen years, I came to a point in my vocational career where I felt a change was needed. During a time when the country was entering the worst economic climate it had experienced since the Great Depression of the 1930's, we took a leap of faith together. It was a moment of truth for us both, one in which I had to practice what I had preached for years; faith requires action. We both felt strongly that we needed to forge a new path in order to be more true to who we were created to be.

Frederick Phillips wrote, "It is often hard to distinguish between the hard knocks in life and those of opportunity."

My wife and I made the daunting decision to make a change that for a season brought about turmoil and upheaval. We stepped out in faith with two small children under two years of age at the time with only our mutual support and strong sense of faith that we could blaze a new trail in life as long as we had each other.

Our parents thought we were not being very practical and responsible in walking away from job security, housing benefits, insurance and pension benefits. We decided to go against conventional wisdom, and we haven't looked back since.

The good news is that we have never been more happy in fulfilled in our marriage than we are now. As we weathered the cocoon stage of our change, we emerged with new wings that enabled us to soar with imagination and creativity. We were blessed and fortunate to have weathered such a dark period of change in our marriage.

Our decision to embrace change became a stepping stone into a brighter future, one filled with hope and possibility. We seized change as an opportunity to make a positive difference in our marriage and for our family. When two people believe in each other anything is possible.

Choose Optimism

The world as we have created it is a process of our thinking. It cannot be changed without changing our thinking.

—Albert Einstein

Change can inspire a *Don't Stop Believing* kind of optimism. On my iTunes playlists, are change-themed songs. A couple of my favorite lyrics is from REO Speedwagon's, *Roll with the Changes*, "I knew we had a heaven, felt the tables turning. Got me through my darkest hour." And the line from Bob Marley's song, *Three Little Birds*, "Don't worry 'bout a thing, 'Cause every little thing gonna be all right."

Right thinking leads to right living. A positive attitude and optimistic outlook is key to viewing life through a lens of hope. It's like putting paint on a canvas and choosing which colors to use. You choose whether to use dark, gloomy colors or bright, inspiring colors with a few pastels thrown in. Your attitude determines whether you view change through a dark and gloomy filter, a vibrant and exciting filter, or a serene and calming filter. The choice is yours.

Bo Bennett wrote, "Having a positive mental attitude is asking how something can be done rather than saying it can't be done."

The temptation to cringe and resist when dealing with change is palpable. Adopting the Hawaiian 'hang loose' mantra when experiencing change is a good place to start. Keeping oneself mentally and physically limber is an effective way to deal with change.

At times, no matter how hard you try to thwart it, change just happens. You can't control it. But what you can control is your response to change. So don't give change any more power over you than it deserves. Along with your partner, be the master of your fate. Hoist the sails and steer change with the rudder of your optimism.

Yes, there will be seasons in your life which will seem pretty bleak. It's during such times that you must become stubbornly optimistic and believe that better times are ahead. You'll be surprised how powerful a positive mental outlook can be in turning a bad situation into an opportunity for a fresh perspective. Optimism knows the sun will eventually shine bright again when the dark clouds dissipate.

Marital Fitness

We first make our habits, and then our habits make us.

—John Dryden

Positive change is often the result of transforming habits. Habits that transform good marriages into great marriages, consist of attitudes and behaviors that nurture love. Transforming habits that

47

strengthen a couple lead to marital fitness.

Marital fitness is accomplished by jettisoning behaviors that are counterproductive to a healthy marriage. Developing new ways of being so that your marriage will thrive, is essential for living heart 2 heart in marriage.

Marital fitness is much like physical fitness. Couples often spend more time, sweat, and money in their personal fitness than they do in their marital fitness. This is one habit that must be tweaked in order for a couple to achieve peak martial fitness.

Dealing with unhealthy habits is essential to a healthy marriage. Just as poor food choices will bring about low energy, lack of desire, and self-loathing. Poor relational habits will lead to low energy in your marriage.

Only when you come to that place where you assume responsibility for your own poor attitudes, poor choices, and poor habits will you find the power to transform. Habits are easy to form and often without conscious awareness, can be incredibly difficult to break.

As with physical fitness so it is with marital fitness. The first step toward developing transforming habits in a relationship is to recognize there is a problem and the problem could very well be your mental attitude. Your partner can't change you no matter how much he or she may strive in fruitless ways to do so. The burden should never be your partner's to shoulder alone in an effort to do the work of two people in keeping a marriage healthy and fit.

Unlike physical fitness, marital fitness takes two and can't be accomplished by only one partner making all the effort. If you become so consumed with your career advancement for example, without consulting and considering your partner's input, your self-serving pursuit could very well bring about a parting of the ways in your marriage. But if you make your hopes and aspirations clearly known to your partner by keeping the communication channels open, you may discover that your partner will be your number one fan, cheering you on to higher and greater success in your career.

Habit transformation is also important to managing familial relationships. Especially early on in your marriage, your primary responsibility is to spend plenty of time cultivating and strengthening your marital relationship. Many couples struggle in this area. How do you juggle your responsibility to your marriage and the creation of a new family it brings about, and scaling back dependence on parents and their expectations of you? Finding that sweet spot is key.

Family fidelity between two partners is just as important as sexual fidelity. Your first commitment and responsibility is to your marriage.

Habit transformation requires adopting new attitudes and behaviors. Discovering what makes you and your partner work in tandem is key to effective habit transformation that will send your marriage soaring to greater heights of fulfillment, satisfaction, and wholeness.

Every couple is different and create a unique chemistry together. What works for one couple may not necessarily work for another couple. One of the reasons is that attitudes and behaviors figure into the relational equation.

Developing a relationship formula that will serve your marriage well, will require adjustments to thinking and living. What may work for John and Sally doesn't mean it will be effective for you and your partner. Discovering what works for your marriage is where the joy in the journey is often experienced. Develop and cultivate relationship-strengthening habits that will make a positive difference in your marriage.

In his book *Anam Cara*, John O'Donohue wrote, "The human journey is a continuous act of transfiguration."

Creating new habits begins with the formation of an attitude that seeks to discover what is gratifying and fulfilling to your partner. When love is reciprocated and two people are working in tandem to create transforming habits together, a marriage becomes the most fulfilling relationship one can ever hope to experience.

Patterns of behavior are telling indicators of probable reactions to future challenges, problems, conflicts, and irritations that life will throw your way. But you don't have to be a slave to behavioral patterns that are unhealthy for a marriage. Adjusting attitudes and making behavioral modifications can empower your marriage to soar.

KISS Exercises

(Keep It Sensible & Supportive)

Rules for Sharing:

Be Open and Honest

Do Not Judge

Respect Your Partner's Thoughts and Feelings

Love Always

1. Discuss what scares you the most about change.

2. Discuss your short term and long term vocational goals.

3. Describe a relationship conflict you've had in the past (with a parent, a prior relationship, friend, or boss). What caused it? How did you respond? Was it ever resolved? If not, why?

4. What kind of attitudes and behaviors could hinder your relationship?

5. Discuss what changes need to take place in your life to make you a better partner in your marriage?

6. Do you view yourself primarily as a positive or negative thinker? Why?

7. What new habits are necessary to make happily ever after a reality for your marriage?

Chapter 4

Being Family

Marriage does not guarantee you will be together forever, it's only paper. It takes love, respect, trust, understanding, friendship, and faith in your relationship to make it last.

—Anonymous

Saying 'I do' on your wedding day, is a promise to create and become a new family with your marital partner. A marriage births a new family dynamic, one in which new traditions and values are established. A new family dynamic will involve compromise and consensus giving rise to hybrid values; a fusion of different values brought into the relationship.

Discussing your values with one another is paramount to keeping your relationship transparent and real. It's important to talk about what worked for you growing up and what didn't work. For example, if your experience growing up was one where your father was the primary bread winner and your mother the primary home maker, then discuss if this model will work in your marriage.

If you grew up in a single parent home, discuss your emotional experiences and what it was like to grow up with only one parent. If you've been in a previous relationship that didn't work out, discuss the reasons why you decided to leave the relationship. More often than not, couples go separate ways because of differing values that were never discussed.

Pay attention to what your partner communicates and take it to heart. Many factors will need to be explored by a couple such as: family upbringing, positive and negative relationship experiences, family traditions, familial values, family planning, financial planning, and any potential differences that will need to be negotiated and managed. Creating a healthy family relationship happens through collaboration, compromise, and cooperation.

Being family involves family fidelity. Practicing family fidelity can prove extremely difficult early in a marriage. Dealing with the relational stress that comes from managing the expectations of in-laws, can be emotionally taxing on a new marriage.

I had a bride-to-be reach out to me prior to her wedding day, voicing concern regarding her fiancé's parents. His parents doted on him. And as such, she felt their relationship was being smothered by her future in-laws. And the fact that he was also employed by them didn't help matters any. Their relationship was beginning to suffer as a result. She desired breathing room so their relationship could bloom and grow.

And although she was also being showered with lots of positive attention by his parents, it was a positive that was quickly becoming a negative. The bride felt strongly that she couldn't, shouldn't, and wouldn't compete for her fiancé's undivided attention.

Their relationship needed their own soil to grow and not the garden soil of his parents. She was developing resentment toward them. It was a crisis serious enough to compel her to seek guidance and counsel in navigating a potential land mine for their future marriage.

The resolution required open and honest communication. By coming together and exploring their feelings on the matter, they were able to address the positive and negative effects of cutting the parental umbilical cord. They also came to understand that it's hard for a parent(s) to release their children into the arms of someone else, allowing for a new family to emerge.

It's difficult for a son or daughter, especially one who has enjoyed a close relationship to a parent(s), to redefine the nature of that relationship after a wedding. But it's absolutely vital that both partners, seeking to create a new family through marriage, do so with sensitivity and respect.

A new family needs plenty of space to breathe and find its own wings without flitting back to mom and dad's home nest for a sense of safety and security. A new marriage will require space to develop and grow. Give your marriage a chance to take root without outside interference.

The temptation when marital problems arise is to run to a parent or guardian. But there is wisdom in not leaning primarily upon parents as the initial go-to-source for counsel. Doing so could unintentionally stir resentment in your parent(s) toward your partner and potentially jeopardize any possibility for a healthy relationship with the in-laws. And resentment could fester in your significant other toward you and your parent(s), as well.

Learning to rely on each other for safety, security, and decision-making is important. But if outside help is needed, professional help and support from peers can prove beneficial. Seeking out a couple that has been married for many years, is a great way to glean advice and receive support during trying times in your marriage.

Being Family Requires Doing

Marriage is not a noun, it's a verb. It isn't something you get. It's something you do. It's the way you love your partner every day.

—Barbara De Angelis

People get married for different reasons. During the initial pre-marital counseling session with a couple, I ask a 'Duh' type of question. "Why do you want to get married?"

Most couples provide the obvious response, "Because we love each other!" And then I follow it up with, "Bless your little hearts. Other than love what else is driving your desire to be married?" And then the real reasons begin to emerge.

Some desire to get married for legal reasons such as military benefits or to secure a mortgage. Some get married because they desire to escape an abusive home environment. Some get married for financial security. Some get married to meet unfulfilled emotional needs — to feel a sense of wholeness again.

Take for example a widow with two young boys. She desperately desires to find someone who can provide financial security, emotional stability, and a father figure for her children. After several years of being alone she feels the weight bearing down on her to provide financial, emotional, and parental security for her kids. She senses her kids fear that something will happen to her leaving them alone and destitute. Thus she handles a date like an interview. Both she and her kids are counting on her to make the right choice.

Regardless of the reasons that motivate an individual to pursue marriage, it's easier to get married than it is to stay married. Forever turns into a long time and the temptation can become great to forsake promises made. But when real love is at the core of the marriage, the promise of 'I do' becomes the marital anthem that is pledged more loudly and sung more lovingly with each passing day.

Empowering Your Marriage

I would say that the surest measure of a man's or a woman's maturity is the harmony, style, joy, and dignity he creates in his marriage, and the pleasure and inspiration he provides for his spouse."

—Benjamin Spock

My wife has played an important part in my personal and professional accomplishments. She has always been a huge supporter and encouragement during times when I would've like to just throw in the towel. One example is when she heard me mention that it would be cool to learn how to fly an airplane. She replied by saying, "Why don't you learn to fly and get your pilot's license." And so I did.

My flight training began at the Dare County Regional Airport (MQI) located on Roanoke Island in Manteo, North Carolina. Learning to fly among some of the most scenic vistas along the outer banks of North Carolina was a life-changing experience.

Due to complex wind conditions along the coast, I learned to fly in less than optimal conditions. It helped make me a safer pilot, one who learned the importance of reviewing weather reports to know when to make a decision to fly or not. A lesson I applied to my marriage. Learn when to speak and when to be quiet and listen.

I learned many lessons from flying that helped me become a better husband and father. One of those lessons was that weight and balance matters. If a plane is overloaded a couple of things happen which could prove fatal. One is that an overloaded plane could fail to gain the necessary lift and stall during takeoff and crash. The other problem that compounds weight overload is that it negatively impacts fuel consumption. A plane in flight that runs out of fuel is a plane with an engine that stops.

Marriage in a similar way requires proper weight and balance. When a relationship is not properly balanced because one person is self-serving, it can prevent a marriage from achieving the necessary lift to take off and soar. It only takes one person to stall a marriage and bring it crashing to the ground.

Many marriages crash and burn during the takeoff phase of marriage. The reason is often due to one person who: tries to control all the decision making, dictate the terms of the marriage, and determine the direction of the marriage. The result is often disastrous to a marriage. You may gain lift on your wedding day, but gaining marital altitude is highly unlikely.

If you want to soar in marriage then establish a healthy relational weight and balance that will keep your marriage primed for flight readiness and maximum fuel economy. A marriage is only as strong as the love and support both partners provide to each other.

The struggle many couples have is making the psychological transition from 'me' to 'we'. While single, the majority of time and energy is self-focused, which is not necessarily a negative thing. But what works when single is not necessarily going to be effective when married.

Much has been written on the topic of psychological empowerment. Some erroneously believe that empowerment is only experienced when one is able to exercise independence and make choices on one's own. Marital empowerment is not achieved in the same way that self-empowerment is achieved.

A huge part of marital empowerment consists of being other-centered, making oneself vulnerable, and being honest with your partner. Some couples choose to put forward only their best face during the courtship for fear of losing acceptance, admiration, and affection. Fear thus establishes the parameters of the relationship, in unspoken ways. The danger is that trust becomes very fragile to the relationship. And once trust is lost in a relationship, it is very difficult to regain.

A healthy marriage begins as a team of two. The core strength and stability of a marriage was established with the promise of 'I do', and it is sustained by an ongoing commitment of two people to live into that promise for the rest of their lives together. 'I do', are two powerful words that can empower a marriage with all that is needed to go the distance and last for an eternity.

Words are powerful. Speaking the right words at the right moment can ignite your marriage with positive energy. Words spoken from the heart, empower and elicit positive energy and inspiration. Learning to speaki the right words with the right tone is like using the correct combination to unlock your partner's heart. When your partner feels valued and respected it will have an empowering effect.

Setting marriage goals and achieving is a great way of empowering your marriage. There is nothing more thrilling than when a team is enjoying a win streak together. But even when goals are not achieved, it can serve as an opportunity to hone your interpersonal skills.

Marital empowerment involves involves adapting to new information, new situations, new environments. Keep the communication channels open and be willing to make necessary adjustments along the way to keep your marriage thriving.

Attitude and outlook is critical. No marriage is perfect because it consists of two imperfect people. Expect let downs, disappointments, and mistakes along the way. Use these as opportunities to make your relationship stronger. Learning to turn a negative into a positive is a sure fire way to empower your marriage.

Be Respectful

The truest form of love is how you behave toward someone, not how you feel about them.

—Steve Hall

Words are cheap. Love is more than a fairy tale where loves true kiss awakens a sleeping beauty from the curse of eternal sleep. And love in a marriage is anything but scripted. Love is nurtured and sustained by certain core values.

Marriages that last consist of the following: respect (caring), responsibility (sharing), empowerment (giving), and resilience (forgiving). Foremost among these core values is respect.

If you treat your partner disrespectfully, you will shut them down emotionally and relationally. Speaking and acting disrespectfully to try and get a point across at the expense of your partner will be counterproductive to nuruturing a healthy a marriage.

A movie I often recommend couples watch is, *A Walk in the Clouds,* starring Keanu Reeves. It's a great love story that it captures the nature of real love and how it grows and flourishes.

Keanu portrays a character named Paul Sutton, who befriends a pregnant woman returning home from college. She has been abandoned by her lover and fearful of her father's reaction. To alleviate her stress, Keanu compassionately volunteers to pretend to be the father of her child and husband.

What ensues is a love story that weaves together the shortcomings and strengths of two very different people from different life experiences and cultures. What begins as a temporary fix, turns into something far more, as love finds intertwines two hearts drawn together by a respect born of love. What Paul Sutton did was honorable and it won the respect of love's true heart. And that's how true love blooms and grows.

Establishing a healthy, blooming marriage is no easy task, but when mutual respect is prevalent all things are possible. Love is born of caring. Love is demonstrated by acts of caring. When you truly care for someone you put that person above your own needs and desires. It's an orientation away from self to the one whom your heart is joined and the one to who you've pledged your love for life.

The simple fact of the matter is that love doesn't just happen. Love matures with time. The heart soil of love is tilled, cultivated and tended by two people on a life journey together. Love takes time to grow, blossom, and flourish. Maturing love is demonstrated by an awareness and respect that gives careful consideration to the thoughts and feelings of one's marital partner.

Hrand Saxenian wrote, "Maturity is the ability to express one's own feelings and convictions balanced with consideration for the thoughts and feelings of others."

Love's true worth emanates from respect. A marital relationship without respect is a marriage that is on borrowed time. If you don't respect someone then your attitude and actions toward that individual are going to be counterproductive to a mutually meaningful and fulfilling relationship. And if two people creating a family together do not share mutual respect then the family is set up for failure.

Nothing will bring a marital relationship crumbling to the ground as quickly as disrespectful attitudes and behaviors. Disrespectful behaviors are often the product of transactional relationships. For example, if the reason for getting married is primarily for financial reasons then the tendency is to treat someone as a means to an end. The absence of respect is a marriage devoid of genuine love born of caring. You will suffer, your partner will suffer, and any children you have will suffer as well. Transactional relationships keep divorce attorneys smiling and busy.

Marriage is more than a mere transaction and your relationship with your partner should demonstrate such. Treating your partner as you would want to be treated is how respect is demonstrated.

Speaking, listening, and behaving with respect, are essential behaviors for keeping a healthy marriage growing in love.

Share Responsibility

It's not someone else's responsibility to honor my marriage. It's my responsibility.

—David Duchovny

A marriage functions best when it's an egalitarian relationship. Sharing responsibilities demonstrates that both partners have bought into the relationship. People tend to take your words more seriously when they know you've got some skin in the game. This begins with sharing the responsibilities that come with being family.

A healthy marriage is one where two people share the responsibilities that come with being family. How will the day in and day out chores be handled? Who will wash and fold clothes? Who will handle the cooking? Who will clean and put away the dishes? Who will be responsible for vacuuming and cleaning the house? Who will handle the grocery shopping? Who will be responsible for handling landscaping and yard management? Will these domestic tasks be a shared responsibility or will there be a clear division of labor? Will there be a six month evaluation of how the domestic responsibilities are being handled; when you sit down together and discuss what's working and what isn't?

Don't sit back and think the two of you will be able to ride along on the coat tails of love. Saying 'I do' will require intentional effort and a lot of hard work to keep the energizer bunny of your marriage hopping along.

Being family is made possible by hearts aligned and atturned; sharing the mutual responsibilities of married life. Love works hard to keep a marriage firing on all cylinders. When a couple is equally dividing up the domestic responsibilities, married life is less of a burden and more of a loving and supportive environment.

Handling Adversity

The oak fought the wind and was broken, the willow bent when it must and survived.

—Robert Jordan, *The Fires of Heaven*

Are you adversity challenged? What is your bounce back rate? How long does it take for you to get back in the saddle after experiencing a failure? Do you manage conflict well? Do you seek to resolve a disagreement fairly quickly or do you like to stew on it for a while? Are you the kind of person that simmers in the juices of bitterness that is seasoned with resentment? Are you quick to throw stones and slow to forgive? Do you tend to fly off the handle when emotionally charged, or do you pause to collect yourself before responding?

Adapting to married life requires a high tolerance for adversity and the ability to respond in appropriate ways. No one is perfect. We're all creatures of emotion and thus will make mistakes along the way. But adjusting attitudes and tempering behaviors will minimize the mess we can often make when flying off the handle.

Being family involves being resilient. Bouncing back from from mistakes is how a married couple weeds the garden of their marriage. Resilient couples are those who enjoy marital longevity.

Nearly every couple that has been married over fifty years were quick to confess that their marriage was far from perfect. What set them apart from couples who divorced is attributed to their resilience. It wasn't because they had less conflict than those who chose to divorce. It was because of their resilience in coming back together and working out the kinks along the way.

When disagreements occur they can sound and feel irreconcilable in the moment. Nothing can be more frustrating and emotionally taxing than when you find yourself at odds with your partner. It's when you feel the painful tip of Cupid's arrow the most. Like a prick in the heart, the object of your affection can do more to set you off than anyone or anything else.

Resilient marriages are those that have mastered the discipline of tempering emotions and possessing a forgiving spirit. There is a a fine line between love and hate. Passion can be so intense that it can quickly go from feelings of love to feelings of hate. Learning to control and calm our emotions is essential to dealing with adversity in marriage.

In his book, *Unapologetically You*, Steve Maraboli wrote, "The truth is, unless you let go, unless you forgive yourself, unless you forgive the situation, unless you realize that the situation is over, you cannot move forward."

Adversity in marriage can be an opportunity to strengthen and deepen your love for each other. Conflict when it is constructive can serve as a positive, fostering greater understanding. It can lead to the kind of relational discovery that enriches and empowers a marriage.

Being family happens when a married couple pull together as one during adversity. The security, stability, and well-being of a family depends upon it.

Honing your relational skills in effectively dealing with adversity will require: tempering your emotional responses, communicating openly and honestly, and practicing reflective listening. There is a lot of mental, emotional, and behavioral work involved in cultivating a healthy, thriving marriage, but it's essential if you plan on expanding your family to include children.

Family Planning

Family isn't always blood. It's the people in your life who want you in theirs; the ones who accept you for who you are. The ones who would do anything to see you smile and who love you no matter what.

—Anonymous

The topic of family planning is one that every couple should discuss. For many couples getting married, they are creating a new family with children from a prior relationship or marriage. Thus it's critically important for a married couple to provide the best possible home environment for children to blossom and grow within.

For others choosing to get married, the hope and promise of having children is palpable. And for some, the idea of having children is frightening and undesireable.

Sharing your hopes and dreams for your marriage and if it will involve having children is very important. If you and your partner do not have children and you desire at some point to do so, discuss your feelings with your partner. When raising the issue of whether to have children or not, opening an honest dialogue tempered with sensitivity to one another's feelings is paramount. Pursuing a marital relationship in which one partner desires children and the other partner doesn't, is setting the marriage up for failure.

Giving careful consideration to the best time to begin having children is also very important. This is an area many couples get ahead of themselves and create unnecessary difficulties. Ideally, it is best if a couple can spend adequate time adjusting to married life before they rush headlong into the parental life.

The best kind of home that you can give a child is one where faith, hope, and love is nurtured. When your marriage is stable and secure, your child(ren) will have the best possible chance to grow within a safe, stable, and secure family environment.

Often when couples begin having children they tend to put their relationship on the back burner. Developing time management skills to juggle parental responsibilities and marital responsibilities will become essential during the early years of raising children.

When a couple fails to focus on their spousal relationship, the entire family suffers. And the effects can be detrimental to the psychological and physical well-being of a child, especially when exposed to a mother and father who incessantly fight, are distant, and unloving to each other. It becomes learned behavior that has damaging consequences for both the short and long term period of your child's life.

Make it a priority to create time and space for you and your spouse to nurture your marital relationship. Date nights with discretionary use of a smart phone, meaning only use in case of an emergency. Social media can become intrusive when you're trying to spend alone time with your partner. It's so tempting to glance down at that message and start tweeting away. Protect your time together and make yourself available only for emergencies.

If you both desire to have children, you will need to discus how your children will be educated and where: public, parochial, or home. Don't take this issue lightly because it involves value choices that often need to be negotiated. The education of children is a matter that you and your partner will need to find common ground, in order to work through any potential differences.

How will corrective discipline be managed in the home? Who will be primarily responsible for the discipline of a child or will this be shared, especially if step-children are involved? Your partner may become very guarded and protective of his/her child when corrective discipline is involved. Discuss some realistic hypothetical scenarios involving the disciplining of a child and how each would handle the situation.

Coming up with a parenting plan with mutually agreeable boundaries for addressing inappropriate behaviors will safeguard a loving home environment.

Blended Families

The secret to blending families is…There is no secret. It's scary and awesome and ragged and perfect and always changing. Love and laugh hard. Try again tomorrow.

—Mir Kamin

With blended family situations, the family dynamic can become complex. Many marriages today are second marriages in which children from a prior relationship(s) are grafted into the new vine. The challenge of balancing relationships with your partner, your step-children, and your own children, can seem daunting, but achieving family harmony is attainable. It just takes time, patience, and a bit of relational common sense.

A marriage that doesn't involve children centers around the couple. When a blended family brings children into the marriage, the family dynamics become vastly different. A marriage that involves children from the outset, are relationship intensive and require a considerable amount of relational effort to make it work for all involved.

Discussing the roles and expectations between a step-parent and step-child is vitally important to establishing effective ground rules and clear parental boundaries.

Within a blended family situation, the tendency is to have unrealistic expectations Having appropriate expectations of your partner is very important. Expecting he/she to become mom or dad overnight is unrealistic. It takes time to establish a bond with a child based on trust, support, and love.

Using effective psychology as a parent and/or step-parent is important in a blended marriage. The following five tidbits of step-parenting advice gleaned from an article on EmpoweringParents.com can save you a lot of heartache if you put into practice.

First of all, especially early on in your marriage let the biological parent deal with disciplinary measures. If you want to get off on the right foot with a step-child then be the good cop and let the biological parent be the bad cop. Things will go much smoother in your relationship with your stepchild when you take a back seat in the area of corrective discipline.

Secondly, be supportive of your partner and don't try to teach him/her "how parenting is really done". Parenting can be very subjective. There is no perfect parent. Encourage and support your partner and try to be less critical and more charitable in your interactions. Having someone who can come alongside and be a steady presence and a caring heart does more to strengthen the bonds of a blended family than anything else you can do.

Thirdly, enter your stepchild's world. Find out what excites him/her. What are his/her interests? Spending time cultivating a heart-felt relationship with your stepchild is also very endearing to the biological parent. It's a great way to bond in your marriage.

Fourthly, respect the time and space between the biological parent and your step-child. Allow them time alone. Early on in a marriage this is very important so that you're not viewed as being in competition with your stepchild. In the long run, this will go a long way toward developing a bond of trust, respect, and love between you and your partner and your stepchild.

Fifthly, don't try to fix your step-child. A child that has experienced the trauma of a divorce or the death of a parent needs to know that they have your full support and love. This will come with time so being present in a supportive role and not in an adversarial role, is how you can best develop a healthy and meaningful long-term relationship with your step-child.

Children are often the innocent ones who suffer the most. By keeping expectations fair and realistic, everyone in the family is provided the grace and patience needed to grow into a cohesive family where everyone feels part of the team.

Managing Finances

No one's achieved financial fitness with a January resolution that's abandoned by February.

—Suze Orman

Financial stress can be an incredible burden on a marriage and the instigator of marital spats. Failing to manage finances can place undue duress on a marital relationship. And the mismanagement of money can become the straw that broke the camel's back for a marriage.

Many couples, young in love, jump in after getting marriage and make big financial decisions. Biting off more than they can chew, their relationship quickly begins to flound. A marriage can suffer unnecessarily, when a couple tries to support a financially burdensome lifestyle.

It's important to discuss how you will manage finances in your marriage. The sooner you can start this conversation the better. If you both have earned incomes then discuss whether there will be joint accounts or separate accounts. If separate, why? How will household expenses be handled?

It's also very important to discuss goals that involve monetary expenditures, whether large purchase items like a house and automobile, or smaller expenditures like family vacations and credit cards. Being on the same page regarding how and when money will be spent, is a very important step toward minimizing financial stress and frustration.

Sharing financial responsibilities is important to the health of a marriage. Money is an area where some couples draw a line in the sand declaring, "This is mine and that is yours." Marriage is a team effort and that involves working together in managing finances.

Love is the great equalizer. It doesn't matter who makes the most money. It's all shared in a healthy marriage.

Prioritizing your spending is very important. For example,

allowing more money in your annual budget to support bonding experiences conducive for long term marital health is highly encouraged. Vacations, mini-vacations, or staycations are great ways to nurture a marital relationship.

My wife and I travelled around the world for nearly five years before we started having children. It was a great bonding time for us. Strengthening your relationship early on in marriage, is very important. Establishing a healthy vacation allowance, if possible, will go a long way toward creating a strong marital bond.

Cooperation is also huge in a marriage. Once you've both communicated openly and honestly, have agreed on goals and how shared resources will be used toward achieving those goals, then it's important that both of you cooperate in the execution of those goals. Nothing can be more frustrating than when two people have agreed on how money is to be spent, and then on a whim, a partner goes off and makes an expenditure that upsets the apple cart.

Money can be such a volatile subject matter in a marriage. It's right up there with politics and religion, requiring a lot of patience, sensitivity, and at times, mitigation by a financial planner. When both partners have agreed on a financial decision, it minimizes the possibility of a blow up. The important thing to keep in mind when trying to effectively manage finances, is to use common sense to avoid breaking the bank.

Be smart about the financial decisions you make. Waiting a year or two on the purchase of a new home or an automobile can help give your marriage the best possible chance of avoiding financial strees early in a marriage.

It's easy to make an impulsive transaction that can take years to get out from under. Losing your marriage and family over mismanaged financies is not worth the risk. Be smart and sensible when it comes to managing your finances together.

KISS Exercises

(Keep It Sensible & Supportive)

Rules for Sharing:

Be Open and Honest

Do Not Judge

Respect Your Partner's Thoughts and Feelings

Love Always

1. Respect is very important in a marriage. How has respect been demonstrated during your courtship? Discuss ways to demonstrate respect in your marriage.

2. Discuss one relational empowerment activity you both will do on a regular basis to strengthen your marriage.

3. Who will handle the domestic responsibilities? Shared? Then discuss how the domestic responsibilities will be handled.

4. Discuss how many children (if any) you both would like to have.

5. If your marriage is a blended family situation, discuss parental expectations in terms of relational bonding, corrective discipline, and education.

6. Discuss how the finances will be managed in your marriage.

7. Discuss ways you both will be intentional about nurturing your relationship including: how many family vacations you plan to take each year, mini-vacations, and/or staycations?

Chapter 5

Core Connections:
Spiritual, Emotional, & Sexual

To live in a peaceful home is to experience paradise on earth.

—Shri Radhe Maa

Feeling a sense of connectedness with your partner is like H2O to a marriage. You can't survice and thrive without it. Being connected in marriage is a state of being where two people are committed to each other's spiritual, emotional, and sexual well-being.

In a blog on Psychology Today, Barton Goldsmith wrote, "Love, intimacy, romance, and sex...are the cornerstones of a loving relationship."

Exercising and strengthening one's relationship core is as important as exercising one's physical core. When a relationship core is strong and functioning in healthy ways, a marriage will continue to flourish. Neglect your relationship and the marriage will begin to wilt on the vine. A weak relationship core fosters a weak marriage.

Spiritual Connection

In order to keep our balance, we need to hold the interior and exterior, visible and invisible, known and unknown, temporal and eternal, ancient and new, together.

—John O'Dononhue

In the movie, *Uncross the Stars*, a grieving husband and his aunt look over a beautiful western landscape. His aunt comments, "This is my favorite spot. Kind of lets you know that God has not taken up all and gone home."

The grieving husband responds, "It's funny to hear you talk about God."

She asks, "Why is that?"

He replies, "You called it a bunch of medieval mumbo jumbo."

She clarifies by saying, "No, I love God. It's his groupies that I have trouble with."

Religion can poison the spirit whereas spirituality breathes life to the soul. One of the reasons that many marriages fail is because they treat it like a religion with unrealistic expectations, social restrictions and relational dogma. The result is that one or both parties within a marriage feels stifled and smothered. There is no joy, no laughter, no excitement. The marriage eventually dies by attrition.

In my book, *Get the Hell Out of Church*, I address destructive attitudes and toxic behaviors that relationally and spiritually tear church communities apart.

The same is true in marriage. In a similar way, a marital relationship can become dogmatic where expectations and desires are imposed on another. When this happens, the spiritual essence of love is diminished and a relationship will suffer.

When one or both partners are consumed with self-centeredness, the marital core of the relationship will suffer and become unstable. Tapping into your spiritual core as a couple will help to center you in your marriage. When you're inner core is quiet and at peace, you are able to cope more effectively when the storms of life blow your way.

Spirituality is more than a state of being religious. Religion is built upon dogma that often does very little to inspire and nurture love, peace, and compassion. Religion often imposes dogma about what we are to do to please God. A spiritual approach focuses more on being rather doing. How am I to respond to God's love, goodness, and compassion?

Marriage is more than an institution; it is a union of love. God is love and so the essence of marriage is love. A spiritual marriage is one where love is a state of being. Spirituality transcends dogma and connects with the Source of all living things. And this is the kind of spirituality that is and vital to relational health and harmony. Spirituality is more than doing; spirituality is being.

The essence of spirituality is experienced in becoming one with God's goodness emanating from his love. It's an energy that flows from the Source of Love through us and in us and all around us.

Ralph Waldo Emerson wrote, "All I have seen teaches me to trust the Creator for all I have not seen."

And so it is in marriage. Seeing and experiencing love in another inspires confidence and teaches one to trust in another. Love is the epicenter of marriage and all things are born and derived from the center. When the spiritual core is stable; the marriage is stable. A marriage that is harmonious is one where a couple has learned to quiet their relational core. It is a peaceful way of seeing and being.

Achieving relational harmony and balance in marriage requires healthy self-renovations. To thrive in a marital relationship, you must first get over yourself. Achieving relational harmony begins with focusing less on self and becoming more attuned to spiritual essence of 'we' in a marriage.

A marriage with a spiritual focus stems from a strong spiritual core. To cultivate and nuture a spiritual aspect to your relationship doesn't require active participation in an organized religious community. For some it helps.

Many couples find spiritual and social support by becoming part of a religious community of faith. This may be the case with you and your partner. Finding common ground upon which to support and sustain your faith values is very important to growing in love as a married couple.

For others, a religious community is a hindrance ot their spiritual growth and well-being. Some of the most spiritual people and loving people I've ever met were not part of organized religion. And some of the least spiritual and self-serving people I've ever met were those immersed in church life and religion.

Environment often shapes behaviors and sadly religious institutions often produce religious people lacking a healthy spiritual core. The world is filled with religion and religious people who are busy doing religious activities. And many of those religious activities may be benevolent or extremely violent. But religion devoid of love does little to achieve spiritual harmony and balance.

Discussing your views on religion and spirituality as a couple is essential, even if you or your partner is an agnostic or atheist. Faith is more than a religious belief system. Whatever orders your life, whatever governs your way of being, is that which you place your faith. Faith can be placed in a deity, ideology, a person, place, or thing.

There are fewer subject matters more controversial than religion. Being honest, open-minded, and respectful in discussing matters of spirituality and religion is important to establishing a stable and secure family.

Over the years I've learned to listen more and judge less when speaking with couples. I'm very respectful of their beliefs. It's obvious that some have really thought through their belief systems. For others, it's an area they haven't really given much thought.

Developing your spiritual life will have the inevitable effect of peeling away the layers of self-centeredness. You will become less preoccupied with self and more focused on what's in the best interest of your marriage. Cultivating spirituality within your relationship will help to shift the focus away from 'my' needs to 'our' needs.

A marriage in balance is one in which both partners are living in spiritual harmony. Life can prove taxing on a marital relationship with all the demands and stresses it imposes. If there is unrest and instability at your core then everything will seem out of kilter. Take the time necessary to ensure that you are calm in your spiritual core.

A few practical ways of cultivating a spiritual life is to take a nature walk together, enjoy a scenic hike on a mountain trail, or a breath-taking stroll along a seashore. Allow nature to open your spiritual senses like Vicks vapor rub opens the sinuses.

Mahatma Gandi wrote, "When I admire the wonders of a sunset or the beauty of the moon, my soul expands in the worship of the creator."

Participating in Yoga together can be effective in helping you as a couple to strengthen your spiritual core. Any activity that relaxes and focuses your mental energy so that all is quiet within, will achieve great dividends in your marriage and professional life. If your spiritual core is calm, you stand a better chance of responding in constructive ways to challenging situations that arise during a marriage.

Emotional Connection

Forgive the past. It is over. Learn from it and let go. People are constantly changing and growing. Do not cling to a limited, disconnected, negative image of a person in the past. See that person now. Your relationship is always alive and changing.

—Brian L. Weiss

Establishing a strong emotional connection in a marital relationship requires a love that forgives wrongs and lets go of the past. Marriage should be a safe haven where two people can build a new future together without the anxiety, fear, or stigma of the past.

What often short-circuits the emotional wiring in a marriage is not something that happens during the marriage but what happened prior to the marriage. Jealousy, unforgiveness, and bitterness can cause a marital partner to feel inadequate, and like water seeping into the crack of a rock, those dark emotions can and eventually break a marriage apart.

A strong emotional connection keeps a marriage on solid ground and foster a healing of the heart and mind. The bonds of marriage require time, love, and tenderness to mature and grow strong. Expecting too much, too quickly in your marriage is a mistake.

Doug Larson wrote, "More marriages might survive if the partners realized that sometimes the better comes after the worse."

Staying emotionally connected requires the following actions: maintain open and honest conversation, talk through unresolved issues, act kindly toward each other, love unconditionally, and never forget that your best friends through thick and thin.

Dr. Brené Brown wrote, To foreclose on our emotional life out of fear that the costs will be too high is to walk away from the very thing that gives purpose and meaning to living."

Learning to trust in love is the key to living heart 2 heart in marriage. An enduring marriage is predicated upon trust. Without trust, every aspect of your relationship will be on shaky ground. Trust is the solid rock that keeps your marriage standing strong when the storms of life threaten.

Ernest Hemingway wrote, "The best way to find out if you can trust somebody is to trust them." It's really that simple. Trust can be unnerving at times. But it is the prerequisite for a loving and lasting marriage.

How do you learn to trust again after you've been burned by someone in a prior relationship? How do you deal with the emotional scarring that often happens due to past hurt and pain? Not easily. But the journey of healing begins with renouncing your fear. You can't get to where you really want to be if you don't take that first step toward your desired destination. Healing begins with learning to trust again by taking one daring step after another.

Freedom in marriage begins from the inside out. When you begin to clear the cobwebs from the closed off places of your heart, you begin to breathe more freely, inhale deeper, and exhale more peacefully. We were all created to dance in the fields of freedom where two people can embrace one another freely and openly in marriage. So don't allow inner demons to deprive you and your partner of a happiness you are meant to enjoy together.

Take time as often as you can, to walk together, talk together, and love together. Create safe spaces where you both can share from the heart.

Sexual Connection

To keep the fire burning brightly there's one easy rule: Keep the two logs together, near enough to keep each other warm and far enough apart — about a finger's breadth — for breathing room. Good fire, good marriage, same rule.

—Marnie Reed Crowell

When emotional distance exists between two people in a marriage, it leads to a lack of desire and intimacy in the bedroom. But when a couple feels a strong emotional connection, their level of intimacy is greater and sexual interactions becomes more meaningful and satisfying. To infuse your marriage with a sex life that is characterized by passion and intimacy, strengthen the emotional core of your relationship.

Sex in marriage is not just about physical bonding but more importantly emotional bonding. When you intimacy is nurtured, the bedroom can become an exciting place to spend quality time with your partner. But when your emotional core is weak or lacking, then don't expect fireworks in the bedroom.

Sometimes it's a real challenge to get on the same page sexually. There are times when a couple go through periods when one desires to make love and the other is just not feeling it. Rather than getting angry and developing feelings of frustration, communicate openly and honestly.

Keeping your sex life active, satisfying, and fulfilling, happens when you and your partner create sparks. What may create sparks for a woman may not necessarily do it for a man. It's important to learn what turns your partner on and off. The emotions are a fragile thing and learning how your partner responds to different triggers is important. Identifying negative triggers that create consternation in your sex life, is important.

I enjoy making a campfire when we spend family time in the Smoky Mountains of Tennessee or making a fire in our firebowl at home. The thing I've learned over the years about building a fire, is that when you have dry wood, a little kindling, a flame starter, and space for air to flow freely, you will have a blazing fire in no time.

It's the same with a passionate sex life. Conditions have to be right. Respect, affection, and admiration do wonders in creating intimacy. Nothing ignites a man's inner fire more than the admiration he receives from his partner. And when a woman feels respected and adored, she is more receptive and responsive in the bedroom.

Learning what creates sparks of desire in your partner is key to enjoying a lifetime filled with passionate and fulfilling sex in marriage. For some it may be the three most powerful words someone can say to another, 'I love you.' Affirming your love for your partner at the beginning and end of the day is a great way to create loving sparks. Doing something that demonstrates you care, is another great way to create some sparks.

Every couple is different. The key is to find out what lights your partner's fire and get about doing just that. We often make marriage more difficult than it really is. Your sex life is an important bonding time between you and your partner. As you grow and mature in your love, the more meaningful your sex life will become in marriage.

Every married couple goes through times in their marriage when making love to each other becomes an effort. Life happens and moods change. Removing self-centered barriers of "my feelings", "my desires", "my life", by treating your partner the way you want to be treated, goes a long way toward strengthening the bonds of matrimony and fostering a healthy sex life in marriage.

Actions speak loudly, and as long as your partner feels respected, admired, and appreciated, your sex life will be more meaningful and satisfying.

KISS Exercises

(Keep It Sensible & Supportive)

Rules for Sharing:

Be Open and Honest

Do Not Judge

Respect Your Partner's Thoughts and Feelings

Love Always

1.   Discuss each other's views about God, Religion, and Spirituality.

2.   What differences in religious and/or spiritual values emerged?

3.   If there are children involved in your marriage or you both are planning to have children, how will religious, spiritual, or non-religious values be instilled during their upbringing?

4.   If you both are planning to raise your children in a faith-based community, discuss the level of participation both feel comfortable with in regards to attendance, joining as members, christening, baptism, or other faith-based practices/rites, etc?

5.   Discuss ways to strengthen the spiritual core of your relationship.

6.   Discuss ways to strengthen the emotional core of your relationship.

7.   Discuss how emotional connectedness is key to a meaningful and satisfying sex life.

Chapter 6

Maturing Love

The best love is the kind that awakens the soul and makes us reach for more, that plants a fire in our hearts and brings peace to our minds, and that's what you've given me. That's what I hope to give to you forever. I love you.

—Young Noah, *The Notebook*

Love is a choice that requires time to grow and mature. Feelings come and go, but a maturing love weathers the harsh trials and travails of life. It's the kind of love that creates relational conditions necessary for a marriage to last.

If a couple can fall in love, they can also fall out of love. Typically what caused you to fall in love is not what's going to keep you in love. Physical attraction and relational chemistry is important, but love encompasses so much more.

Understanding the maturing nature of love is critical to having a realistic perspective about marriage. So how does a couple avoid becoming a divorce statistic? It's really simple – by maturing in love.

An emotion-based marriage burns out fast. Feelings can be misleading. Love is a choice and activates the inner drives of longing, determination, and resilience. Love inspires hopeful expectation that all things can and will work out for the best, when two people keep faith in each other.

It's perfectly normal to have feelings of melancholoy in a relationship. It doesn't mean that your love is dying or that you should give up on your marriage. Every relationship goes through growing pangs where the marriage is maturing in love. It's important not to become reactive and make emotion-based knee-jerk reactions. The exact opposite is required.

Thinking-based relationships are proactive and know when to have fragile emotions to take a backseat to reason. Sometimes your emotional life needs to be given a timeout, in order to put an issue in perspective. Reason can bring clarity whereas emotions can cloud judgment.

Rarely is it ever a good thing to make a knee-jerk reaction when emotionally charged. And yet as creatures of emotion, we are prone to speak and say things we don't mean and can't take back. When you allow your emotions to get ahead of clear thinking, you may end up compounding and escalating a sensitive issue rather than defusing it.

Tempering emotions with appropriate responses that are not disproportionate to the situation will lead to a stronger marriage. By working through disagreements, concerns, and challenges, you begin to demonstrate a mature love that makes a marital relationship more supportive and healthy.

Love is the great architect of the heart. It inspires, enables, and empowers. When mature love is reflected in a marriage, possibilities are inspired, potential is unleashed, and goals achieved. The kind of love that is uplifting and compelling is the stuff of real love, where two people are completely devoted to each another.

Growing in Wisdom

Speak when you are angry and you will make the best speech you will ever regret.

— Ambrose Bierce

Maturing love is characterized by wisdom. Become wise in the matters of the heart. It's like having a flashlight to navigate in a dark house. Without wisdom you will find yourself bumping frustratingly along as you walk into wall after wall of marital spats and disagreements.

Wisdom empowers a couple to know when to speak, when to listen, and when to take a time out. When people are emotionally charged the tendency is to say spiteful words and make irrational decisions. Learning to address issues that arise between you and your partner in a civil and respectful manner, is vital to an emotionally stable and healthy marriage.

Disagreements happen in relationships. The challenge is to

effectively deal with disagreements when they do. Agreeing on taboo behaviors for your marriage can help establish boundaries that will safe guard your relationship. And one such taboo should be that neither you nor your partner should use disparaging words when speaking to the other. If you don't have something constructive to say then don't say it.

The old children's nursery rhyme simply isn't true, "Sticks and stones may break my bones but names will never hurt me." Words do hurt. The more hateful the words, the more destructive they are. Words are palpable and when used maliciously, they can elicit destructive reactions that can bring a relationship to ruin.

Words wound and lead to emotional scarring that often permanently damage individuals and relationships. Wisdom and self-control go hand and hand. Think before speaking is a habit to master in a marriage. And learning to speak the right words is essential to maintaining relational health.

Experience, knowledge, and good judgment go along way toward working the kinks out of a marital relationship. It takes time to grow in love, and with experience we begin to learn how to smooth out the rough edges of our relationship.

Our daughter Kiera came home from school one day and said, "There are not winners and losers. There are only winners and learners." It's a lesson she learned from her third grade teacher. What a great lesson to learn in a marriage as well. We all make mistakes and just because we do, doesn't make us a loser or failure in a relationship. The important thing is to learn from our mistakes so we can avoid making them again.

Wisdom is knowledge and knowledge is power. When you invest your time, energy, and resources into embodying marital wisdom, you will love more deeply, feel more compassionately, and understand more empathetically.

Growing in Understanding

One of the best things about love—the feeling of being wrapped, like a gift, in understanding.

—Anatole Broyard

Within all of us is an innate desire to be loved and understood. A healthy, loving relationship involves real connection, meaninfgul interactions, romantic imagination, and deep understanding. To be known and understood by your partner brings with it a depth of love that fosters trust, respect, and admiration. A lasting connection is established between two people when they've spent quality time getting to know one another.

Maturing love involves getting to know the many facets of your partner including: upbringing, life experiences, passions, goals, and values. When you genuinely care enough about your partner, you take time to understand, affirm, and embrace your partner who they are rather than for who you desire them to be.

Understanding your partner is the prerequisite to truly living heart 2 heart in marriage. And it is the key to marital longevity that will lead you to your happily ever after. The married life can be fulfilling when two people have taken the time to cultivate a relationship built on mutual understanding. Nothing is less satisfying than living with someone who does not get you.

When two people take the time to get to know one another a strong bond who cultivated. The result is an understanding that speaks the language of love. It's like going to another country when you know their culture, respect their values, and understand their history. A warm welcome is usually the response. It's the same with a marriage. Your partner desires to be understood and respected for who they are, not what you wish them to be.

Steve Maraboli wrote, "When you say 'I' and 'my' too much, you lose the capacity to understand the 'we' and 'our'."

When you understand someone else, you will find yourself judging less and appreciating more. It requires patience and sensitivity. Learn to listen to your partner without rushing to judgment.

Understanding comes down to desire. How much do you really desire to understand your partner? It's freeing to know your understood and valued by someone you love. It ignites a burning fire in the heart when two souls are intertwined in genuine love. To understand and to be understood, leads to a depth of sharing that takes a marriage to a whole new level of intimacy and satisfaction.

Growing in Togetherness

When we honestly ask ourselves which person in our lives means the most to us, we often find that it is those who, instead of giving advice, solutions, or cures, have chosen rather to share our pain and touch our wounds with a warm and tender hand.

—Henri Nouwen

Love involves caring enough to share. This is the essence of togetherness. When you're truly together in a marriage, the two become one. It's one of the fundamentals of a healthy marriage. When you love someone, you demonstrate it by your actions.

Sharing dreams, responsibilities, and burdens, creates a cohesive bond that brings equilibrium to a marriage. The weight of everyday tasks become more easier to bear when two people share the load. Life becomes more bearable when two people work together in making a marriage the best it can be.

Togetherness is about establishing a culture of sharing in your marriage. By learning to harmonize the yin and yang of a relationship, a couple enjoys a healthy balance where both are working in concert. During the turbulence of life, it is great to know that your not alone.

Togetherness is a kinship of heart that breathes life into your soul. It establishes a strong foundation in your marriage. And it bears the fruit of a happy marriage and a lasting love and an enduring love.

Mastering REAL

Authenticity is a collection of choices that we have to make every day. It's about the choice to show up and be real. The choice to be honest. The choice to let our true selves be seen.

—Brené Brown

In her book, *The Velveteen Rabbit*, Margery Williams writes the following scene, "Real isn't how you are made,' said the Skin Horse. 'It's a thing that happens to you. When a child loves you for a long, long time, not just to play with, but REALLY loves you, then you become Real.'

'Does it hurt?' asked the Rabbit.

'Sometimes,' said the Skin Horse, for he was always truthful. 'When you are Real you don't mind being hurt.'

'Does it happen all at once, like being wound up,' he asked, 'or bit by bit?'

'It doesn't happen all at once,' said the Skin Horse. 'You become. It takes a long time. That's why it doesn't happen often to people who break easily, or have sharp edges, or who have to be carefully kept. Generally, by the time you are Real, most of your hair has been loved off, and your eyes drop out and you get loose in the joints and very shabby. But these things don't matter at all, because once you are Real you can't be ugly, except to people who don't understand."

***

The acronym REAL (Romance, Encourage, Affirm, Love) is a memorable way to remember the essential keys to lasting and meaningful intimacy.

Always make time to ROMANCE your partner. An ongoing romantic relationship keeps the heart fire of a marriage burning strong. Often after the courtship it's the romance that seems to get left out in the cold.

Marriage is when romance should be the rule rather than the exception. Romance is like the seasoning on your favorite foods. It's the floral scent that entices the senses. To romance your partner is to make him/her feel special.

Don't become a dullard in your marriage. Put some flamboyance in your relationship and share a good laugh that makes the heart smile. Affirming words and loving actions is like fertilizer to a marriage. It will draw you closer together and strengthen the marital bond.

Be intentional about seeking to ENCOURAGE your partner. We all could use some encouragement. Life is tough at times. We all get down, feel discouraged, and defeated. It's during such times that a timely word or empathetic hug can turn a downer of a day into an uplifting and motivating moment for your partner.

Encouragement is medicine to the soul and lifts the spirit. A friend who comes along and encourages you when you need it most is a friend you want to keep around. And that's what a marriage partner is – a keeper. An encouraging word is provides the much needed motivational boost for someone to clear a hurdle in life.

Encouragement inspires confidence, provides support, and offers hope to another. When encouragement becomes a way of being in your life, it will keep your partner coming back for more. Encouragement is intoxicating – it draws, compels, and energizes.

Make it a daily habit to find something to AFFIRM about your partner. Affirmation is important to nurturing one's emotional well-being. We all need it and we all should receive it, especially from our marriage partner.

Tia Walker wrote, "Affirmations are our mental vitamins, providing the supplementary positive thoughts we need to balance the barrage of negative events and thoughts we experience daily."

Negativity is a drain that saps our emotional energy. When negativity creeps into a marriage, it can erode and rend asunder the bond of marriage. Recognize dark thoughts and negative behaviors and avoid both at all costs

Affirmation acts as a preventative agent that clears the air of negativity. When you speak positive things about your partner, it infuses your marital relationship with positive energy. It brings about positive karma. What you sow, you shall reap.

Make it a habit to begin each day by saying something affirming that makes your partner feel important, valued, and respected. The lack of affirmation can emotionally cripple someone. And it can cripple a marriage.

To affirm is to love. The more affirming your are, the more loving you become. They both go hand in hand.

And the foundation of any marriage is LOVE. When you said, 'I do!' at the wedding altar, you were making a promise to love your partner with all your heart, mind, soul, and strength. Psychological health and sense of wholeness within a marriage, is closely linked to the feeling of love and acceptance by a significant other.

Maya Angelou wrote, "Love is that condition in the human spirit so profound that it allows me to survive, and better than that, to thrive with passion, compassion, and style."

Love is compelling when two people commit to love each other regardless of the baggage, annoying behaviors, differing values, or peronsal idiosyncrasies. When you truly love another and receive love from another, nothing seems insurmountable.

Often in marriage when issues arise the tendency is to magnify them into a win/lose situation. Rather than focusing on winning an argument, a couple should focus on losing more often. We all need to lose our stubbornness, lose our pride, lose our selfishness, and lose our entitlement thinking.

When you lose in love, your marriage wins. When loving becomes more important than winning, you will experience what it is to mature in love.

KISS Exercises

(Keep It Sensible & Supportive)

Rules for Sharing:

Be Open and Honest

Do Not Judge

Respect Your Partner's Thoughts and Feelings

Love Always

1. How well do you know your partner? Share something you're partner may not know about you.

2. What are your partner's goals, aspirations, and dreams?

3. Discuss the importance of having a deeper level of understanding about each other.

4. Do you consider yourself a giver or taker by nature? Write a list of behavior patterns and categorize either as giving or taking. Which is dominant in your life?

5. How are you both currently growing in wisdom, understanding, and sharing? How is your relationship demonstrating signs of maturing? What areas are demonstrating immaturity?

6. Discuss the acronym REAL. How are you both currently romancing, encouraging, affirming, and loving each other in your relationship.

7. Discuss what it means to lose in love in order to win in marriage. What compromises are required to make your marriage last?

Chapter 7

Living Happily Ever After

To commit to loving a person for five minutes is easy. To commit to loving a person for the rest of your life…is a strong commitment.

—Tom Houck, *Being Faithful To Your Future Spouse*

I came across an anonymous quote recently on social media, "Family. Where life begins. And love never ends." Happily ever after is for some an idealistic notion that is the stuff of fairy tales. For others it's the pursuit of a way of life where dreams come true.

I believe happily ever after is a love story being written daily by two people who are committed to pulling together, dreaming together, and growing together in love. It's a shared journey where the power of love teaches, shapes, and infuses a couple with a sense of wonder and possibility.

Fairy tales evoke our deepest sense of longing. Everyone longs to be loved. We were created to love and be loved. Love is a powerful human emotion and can be transformative. But love is more than a magic wand.

Love struggles. Love struggles to win, struggles to rise, and struggles to be.

Living into one's happily ever also requires a lot of hard work. It isn't easy because neither you nor your partner is perfect. You both will make mistakes. And love doesn't always feel happy. There will be times during your marriage when you will feel crappy rathet than happy.

Marriage can get ugly, life can become a downer, and your heart light will grow dim. Negative thoughts can creep in and doubt may cloud your judgment. You may even question after the fact, whether your marital partner is the right person for you.. But during such times you must rid your mind of all doubt.

In his book, *Venus in Arms*, Criss Jami wrote, "To say that one waits a lifetime for his soulmate to come around is a paradox. People eventually get sick of waiting, take a chance on someone, and by the art of commitment become soulmates, which takes a lifetime to perfect."

Love is more than a feeling, it is loyalty, patience, persistence, and commitment. The promise you made to your partner on your wedding day must be reaffirmed throughout your marriage. It is a daily commitment to stick together through sickness and health, good times and bad, and for better or worse.

Love and commitment go hand and hand. Commitment is a word seldom used and seldom valued. We live in a culture that would rather talk about freedom from commitment rather than freedom in commitment. Some avoid the married life because they fear the responsibilities and obligations it entails.

Commitment in marriage means different things to different people. There are numerous reasons why people desire to be in a committed relationship and thus pursue marriage. Promising 'I do' to another is easy. Making good on that promise is separates real love from a fantasy bond.

For some, commitment means fidelity to a religious vow. To break faith with one's partner is to break faith with God. But commitment to a partner in marriage must be stronger than a sense of obligation to a religious vow. Otherwise, a marriage can go from bond to bondage if religion is the reason one seeks to remain married. Even God recognizes the hollowness of a hypocritical relationship that merely gives lip service for the sake of religion when the heart is not involved (Isaiah 29:13).

For others, commitment in a marriage is measured by self-serving ends. As long as the marriage meets expectations, the commitment is worthwhile. But once the marriage doesn't serve those ends, 'I do' quickly becomes 'I don't!' Some people seek marriage only for financial gain. Commitment to financial security is the primary motivation. As long as a partner is financially towing the line, all is well. But if fortunes change due to unforeseen and uncontrollable situations such as an economic recession, demotion, or loss of job; the marriage vows no longer hold sway over one's sense of commitment to the marital relationship. Take away the financial support and the sense of commitment greatly diminishes.

Like the man who told his friends about his divorce, "Yeah, she divorced me for religious reasons. She worshipped money and I didn't have any."

For others commitment in marriage is only as strong as the sex life. Their commitment is to the bedroom. As long as the sex is good, commitment is not a problem. But as goes the sexual passion, so goes the marraige.

Being committed involves so much more. Commitment in a marital relationship should never be primarily about self, religion, finances, or sex. Commitment in a marital relationship is rooted in love and not personal gain.

A committed marriage involves two people who are ONE in heart and life. When two people embody the essence of love they demonstrate what it means to live heart 2 heart in marriage. Let's examine some of the distinctive marks of a committed marriage.

Collaboration & Cooperation

So it's not gonna be easy. It's gonna be really hard. We're gonna have to work at this every day, but I want to do that because I want you. I want all of you, forever, you and me, every day.

—Young Noah, *The Notebook*

Collaboration is a mark of a committed marriage. Lasting marriages are by those who have learned the art of collaborating by:

- Finding common ground when addressing ideas and goals.

- Practicing reflective listening to validate your partner's contributions.

- Being generous with compliments.

- Keeping a sense of humor.

- Avoiding putting results before relationships.

- Agreeing to disagree when necessary to move beyond impasses.

- Always thinking prior to speaking so that you don't put your foot in your mouth.

- Encouraging participation so both take ownership of the resolution.

- Not taking differences of opinion personally, but rather focus on the ideas being discussed.

- Not trying to be right all the time.

Working together to make your marriage work also requires cooperation. A marriage can quickly turn into a tug of war contest with two people pulling against the other. But when a couple live and love in a spirit of cooperation, they navigate relational tension by achieving consensus through compromise.

There will be times in your marriage when you will not see eye to eye with your partner. And differences of opinion, values, or goals can become larger than life. As Bruce Springsteen s ings in the *Tunnel of Love*, "You got to learn to live with what you can't rise above."

Developing a culture of cooperation in your marriage takes time to cultivate. A great way to hone your cooperation skills is to find a fun activity that you both enjoy doing together that requires a high level of interaction. If you live near water then I highly recommend kayaking.

My wife and I enjoy two person kayaking. It's a recreation activity where we have to paddle in tandem to keep ourselves heading in the right direction. Early on in our kayaking adventures we discovered that without synchronizing our oar strokes in the water we would expend a lot of energy twisting and turning in directions we didn't realize a kayak could go in. When we learned to work in concert with each other, the kayaking experience became most enjoyable.

When we first began kayaking together in one kayak, we experienced a lot of frustration and shared some laughs. But with time, we honed our collaboration and cooperation skills. And now kayaking together is a blast.

Kayaking together, like being married, is great way to work through the kinks of what it entails to be on the same team. Collaborative skills in marriage has innumerable benefits such as clarifying objectives, managing finances, establishing expectations and boundaries with extended family, sharing domestic responsibilities, raising kids, and career decisions.

The signs leading to your happily ever after are labeled collaborate and cooperate. It's so easy for two people to lose each other in marriage, but it doesn't have to be that way. Your ability to collaborate and cooperate will determine to a large extent whether you will succeed or fail in your relationship.

Finding Grounds for Marriage

In every marriage more than a week old, there are grounds for divorce. The trick is to find, and continue to find, grounds for marriage.

—Robert Anderson, *Solitaire & Double Solitaire*

Three days after I officiated a wedding for a couple, I received a call from the groom. He asked if I had already mailed the marriage license back to the probate court, which I had. He was hoping that I hadn't. When I asked if anything was wrong he despondently answered, "I don't think this is going to work out." After only a few days he was already willing to call it quits. Not a young groom but rather one mature in years, he was one who had taken meticulous efforts to plan every detail of his wedding, but had given little preparation for the marriage.

Couples often take their marriage for granted and invest little effort in finding grounds for marriage. It's easy to find reasons to quit and just give up. We learn this defeatist skill early in life. But learners and winners find ways to succeed.

To succeed in marriage, you will need to prepare and work hard at marital fitness. It's not going to be easy. You must invest in your marriage as much as you do in your career, your health fitness, or your stock portfolio. Standing by your partner and investing in your relationship is what great marriages are made of.

Gordon B. Hinckley wrote, "The remedy for most marital stress is not in divorce...It is in simple integrity that leads a man and a woman to square up their shoulders and meet their obligations. It is found in the Golden Rule, a time-honored principle that should first and foremost find expression in marriage."

Attitude is everything in a marriage. When you keep a positive outlook and seek ways to work through the tough times, a marriage will stand the test of time. A tough as nails mentality will do wonders for a couple who are committed to their marital relationship.

Keeping your wits about you during marriage is also very important. Recognizing the need for cooling off space during a disagreement minimizes the possibility of rifling off words that could leave emotional scarring. It's always best to speak from a settled heart rather than from reckless lips. A wise person once wrote (Psalm 141:3 NIV), "Set a guard over my mouth, LORD; keep watch over the door of my lips."

Choosing to speak words that build up your partner can make all the difference in your marriage. There will be no shortage of harsh words that will flood your thoughts in the heat of anger. You can think it, but don't say it. Once an arrow is unleashed from the bow it can't be recalled. The damage is done. Practice self-control and take a time out during disagreements to avoid speaking words you may regret.

Adversity often reveals one's true character. But that isn't necessarily a bad thing. We all have personal edges that need to be refined. Keep an open mind and teachable spirit so that you can learn from your mistakes and become a better partner, lover, and companion in marriage.

The power to choose is a freedom that one exercises in a relationship. Remaining married is a choice, just as choosing to get a divorce is a choice. The difference between a couple that chooses divorce and a couple that chooses to remain married, comes down to loyalty, integrity, and love.

Barring justifiable reasons to end a marriage, such as loss of trust emanating from adultery or loss of respect emanating from verbal or physical spousal abuse, many couples choose to end their marriage due to selfish reasons that demonstrate a lack of commitment to love. Love is more than a feeling, it's a choice that requires commitment, sacrifice, and perseverance.

There are many reasons that couples who were once happily married give for getting a divorce. The following is a sampling of reasons of why some people choose to get a divorce.

- Some feel they're not meant to be with their partner anymore.

- Some feel they're not cut out for a monogamous relationship.

- Some feel that time creates changes in themselves and their partner resulting in a growing apart.

- Some feel that they're simply not getting enough sex.

- Some feel they've lost hope in themselves, in their partner, or in life.

• Some feel the blinders were pulled back revealing a stranger they never knew existed.

• Some just got tired of dealing with the lack of respect and disdain felt from their in-laws.

• Some were unwilling to subject themselves any longer to the expectations of another person.

A couple must have a "we're in it to win it" attitude about marriage. And a winning attitude involves a commitment to preparation. If you don't take the time to prepare and invest in your relationship then you cheat your marriage. Nothing of any significance has ever been gained from a lack of preparation.

Some people enjoy the benefits of marriage but do not want the responsibilities that come along with One doesn't have to think long or wait long to come up with a reason to convince oneself that choosing to get a divorce is the best solution to relationship that has become frustrating and dissatisfying. That's a defeatist attitude. it.

An anonymous source once said, "A perfect marriage is just two imperfect people who refuse to give up on each other." Authentic love tows the line and works at forgiveness and reconciliation. Love takes time to mature. When two people who are committed to each other in marriage give love a chance to blossom and grow, love will begin to work its magic.

Making Marital Magic

All the world is made of faith, and trust, and pixie dust.

— J.M. Barrie, Peter Pan

There is something magical about the allure of happily ever after that inspires a couple to lean in a little closer, hope a little harder, believe a little more. We all yearn to be loved, accepted, and affirmed for who we are and for what we might become. Think of the power two people would possess together if they loved each other this way. Power to achieve goals, to reach a greater sense of meaning, to pursue new possibilities, to explore and discover the wonders that only love can reveal.

Marriage is not a destination but a journey. Couples often forget this fact. The goal in any relationship, and especially in marriage, is to be the best partner you can be. It's an attitude of the heart that settles for nothing less than perfection in love.

Striving to love someone unreservedly, unconditionally, and completely is the goal in a marriage. To fully give yourself to loving another is what real passion is all about. There is no greater thrill than being swept along in marital love affair where beauty and serenity envelop you with positive, flowing energy?

The power of love casts its own magical spell over a couple. It's the promise of commitment that chooses to say, 'I do," each and everyday of one's married life. And the longer you continue to say those two words to each other, the more magical your married life will become.

Making marital magic is more than enjoying lots of sex or feeling happy. Marital magic is a relational energy that is so potent between two people that it creates a vibe of heart and life that makes the unseen seen, the seen disappear, and the impossible possible. It's a chemistry of the heart that channels the passion of mind and body, inspiring a transforming love that is experienced and expressed through marriage.

Robert Craig Clark wrote, "Beyond all reason is the mystery of love."

Marital magic defies the odds, challenges conventional thinking, and embraces the unknown. And therein lies the secret to making marital magic; defying one's reason, one's senses, one's fears. by living into the promise of 'I do!'

Touch the heart and you will tap a well-spring of love that will flow eternal. Marital magic is experienced through the power of two souls knit together in mind, body, and spirit. They are connected in an unforgettable and never-ending journey of love. Through the power of physical and spiritual connectedness, two souls truly become one in marriage.

Saying 'I do' is a admirable promise. It will require grit and an imagination that sees nothing but wide open spaces of possibility for you and your partner. Set-backs, obstacles, and annoyances will come your way in marriage. Count on it.

The temptation will be to give in and give up on your love.

Resist the easy way out. Choose to face your trials, frustrations, and disappointments with hope. Be a winning team that prepares for success and is determined to go the distance. Together you will stand in marriage but apart you will fall in divorce. Choose to stand.

Your wedding day began an exciting new chapter in your life. Your marriage is the love story you both will create together with many new and exciting chapters to be written. Set the tone and trajectory of your life by choosing to put love first in order to make love last.

I like the anonymous quote that states, "We may not have it altogether, but together we have it all."

Make your love story an exciting and magical one. A story with just the right amount of faith, trust, and pixie dust to transport you to your happily ever after. And it all begins with saying, 'I do!'

KISS Exercises

(Keep It Sensible & Supportive)

Rules for Sharing:

Be Open and Honest

Do Not Judge

Respect Your Partner's Thoughts and Feelings

Love Always

1. Discuss with your partner the implications of being committed to your relationship and marriage?

2. Discuss practical ways to invest in your marriage so as to maximize your return on investment in terms of relational fulfillment, mutual satisfaction, and marital longevity.

3. Are you the kind of person that likes to be right all the time? If so, how will you become intentional about respecting your partner's opinions?

4. What are some practical ways that you can demonstrate your love to your partner?

5. Discuss the importance of collaboration and cooperation in your marriage.

6. Discuss your hopes and dreams for living a real-life love story together for the rest of your lives.

7. Discuss ways you both will create marital magic together.

MORE BOOKS BY HOLT CLARKE

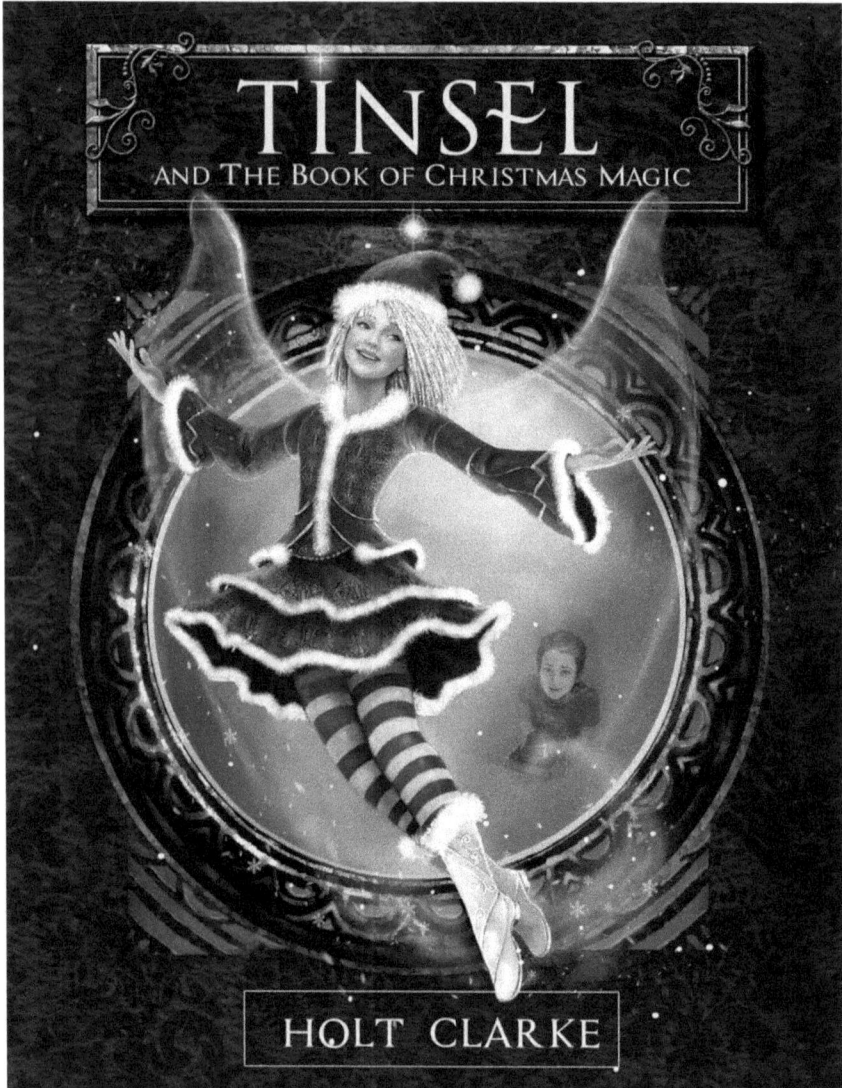

Visit HoltClarke.com

TINSEL
AND THE CHILD OF LIGHT

HOLT CLARKE

Visit Holtclarke.com

Santa Claus

and the
Kingdom
of
Christmas

HOLT CLARKE

Visit HoltClarke.com

Visit HoltClarke.com

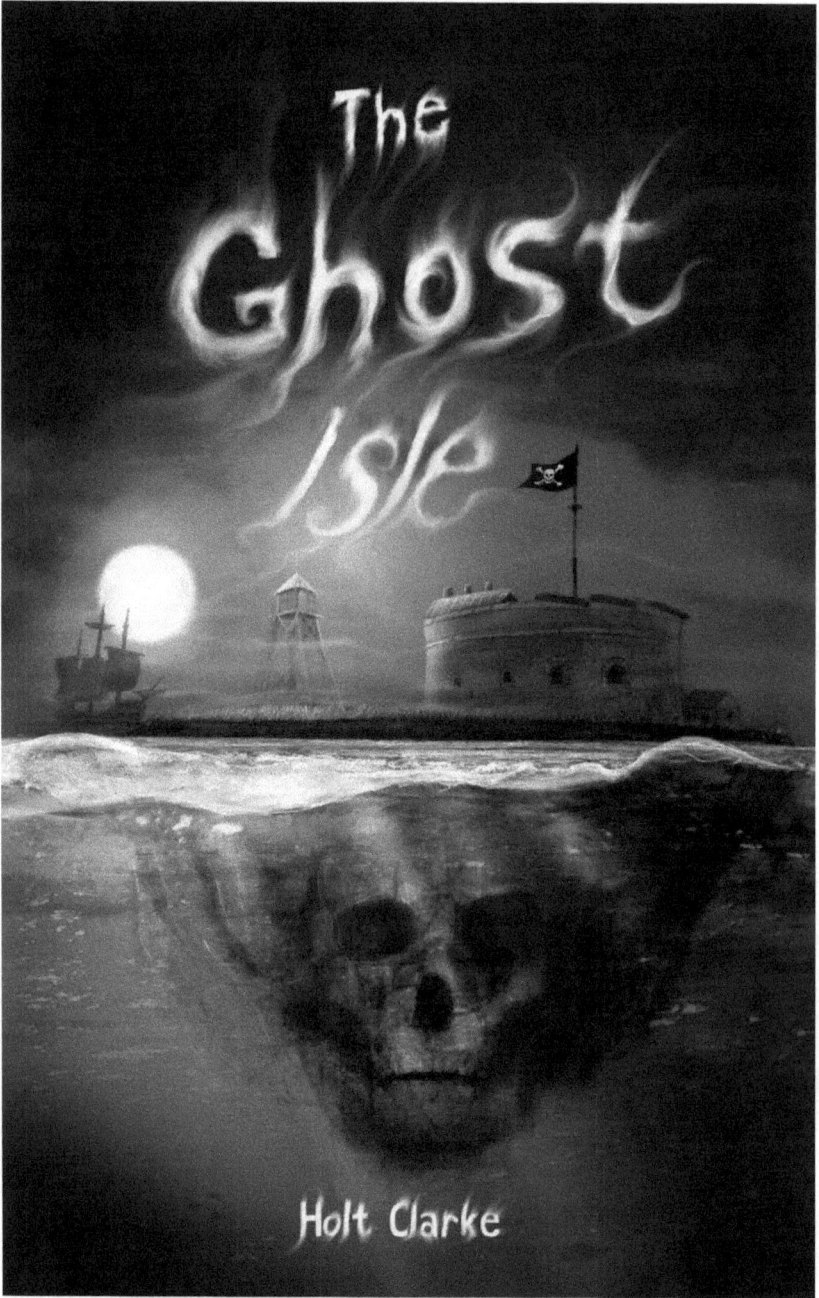

The Ghost Isle

Holt Clarke

Visit HoltClarke.com

SWITCHING MAMA'S ASHES

MAMA
R.I.P

HOLT CLARKE

Visit HoltClarke.com

HOLT CLARKE

THE SWORD OF EDEN

Visit HoltClarke.com

Seanna
and
the
Magic
Moon

KIERA CLARKE

Visit KieraClarke.com

Boys Are
Sooo
Annoying

Kiera Clarke

Visit KieraClarke.com

ABOUT THE AUTHOR

Dr. Holt Clarke is a destination wedding minister and marriage coach. He is also an author of imaginative fiction. Happily married and Dad to the coolest kids on earth, Dr. Clarke is a regular on Santa's Nice List, and keep'n the magic real with his family in Charleston, South Carolina.

Holt earned the Doctor of Ministry degree from Drew University, Master of Divinity degree from Duke University, and Bachelor of Arts degree from North Carolina Wesleyan College.

Visit HoltClarke.com for news and updates.

SPONSORED BY

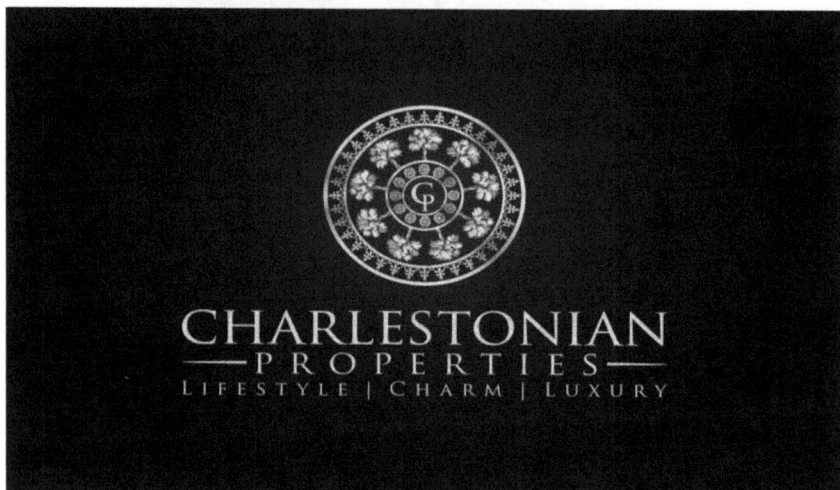
SUPPORTING THE LITERARY ARTS

CharlestonianProperties.com

www.ingramcontent.com/pod-product-compliance
Lightning Source LLC
Chambersburg PA
CBHW072144020426
42334CB00018B/1886